CONQUER DISCIPLINE

THE MAGIC OF CREATING MENTAL TOUGHNESS,
FREEDOM & BECOMING THE BEST YOU!

N.M. HILL

© **Copyright N.M. Hill 2021 - All rights reserved.**

The content contained within this book may not be reproduced, duplicated, or transmitted without direct written permission from the author or the publisher.

Under no circumstances will any blame or legal responsibility be held against the publisher, or author, for any damages, reparation, or monetary loss due to the information contained within this book. Either directly or indirectly. You are responsible for your own choices, actions, and results.

Legal Notice:

This book is copyright protected. This book is only for personal use. You cannot amend, distribute, sell, use, quote, or paraphrase any part, or the content within this book, without the consent of the author or publisher.

Disclaimer Notice:

Please note the information contained within this document is for educational and entertainment purposes only. All effort has been executed to present accurate, up to date, and reliable, complete information. No warranties of any kind are declared or implied. Readers acknowledge that the author is not engaging in the rendering of legal, financial, medical, or professional advice. The content within this book has been derived from various sources. Please consult a licensed professional before attempting any techniques outlined in this book.

By reading this document, the reader agrees that under no circumstances is the author responsible for any losses, direct or indirect, which are incurred as a result of the use of the information contained within this document, including, but not limited to, — errors, omissions, or inaccuracies.

DEDICATION

To my beautiful mum (Jamila) who is no longer with us.

The way my mum lived her life she was the epitome of discipline.

We miss you.

CONTENTS

Introduction — 7

1. What is discipline? Is it even important? — 13
2. Motivation - no thanks, I'm dandy — 30
3. What Goes In Must Come Out — 50
4. Free As A Bird — 69
5. Cohabit With Habits — 88
6. A million dollars today or a penny a day doubled for 30 days? — 110
7. Valentine's day - all day, every day — 130
8. Move The Needle — 148
9. Magic Mindset — 170

Conclusion — 193
Spread The Word — 207
References — 209

INTRODUCTION

Discipline is one of the key foundation blocks of personal development. Learning how to conquer it and use it can change your life. This book will explain the best methods to use and how you can apply them without stress. Learn how to make instant changes as you work your way through the book. Start to embrace change and enjoy long-term, positive effects.

You will learn how to flip a negative into a positive in only a few seconds. Discover how to control your thoughts and stay positive in challenging times. Also, how to organise your time to become more proactive and productive. The possibilities are endless when you know how to make the right choices.

Your journey will be mind-blowing.

If you are reading this introduction, you already want to create a better life for yourself. Personal development is life-changing and can open up your life to endless opportunities. You might currently feel stuck and wonder what else you can achieve. Mental discipline gives you the control box to make your dreams a reality.

If the following situations sound familiar, this book will be invaluable to you.

- You like to start new projects but get frustrated when you struggle to finish them.
- You are a master procrastinator who finds distractions everywhere.
- Negative imposter syndrome thoughts stop you from moving forwards with your dreams.
- You are always in a rush and find it challenging to manage your time.
- The idea of doing something outside of your comfort zone scares you.

THE BODY AND MIND CONNECTION

Think about everything that you do to look after your body. You eat well and exercise to keep yourself in shape. But do you do anything to look after your mind? When you have both a healthy body and mind, it takes things to the next level. It is a perfect alignment that attracts more extraordinary things.

Mental practices that discipline your mind can give you mental toughness. You can start to control your life instead of running around in circles. Set goals, work towards them, and achieve them. Then repeat the process to keep creating the best version of yourself.

You will feel like a sponge, taking in more water as you grow.

The beauty of personal development is you don't need any previous experience or training. You only need two things: an open mind and a readiness to change your life forever.

One of the pioneers of personal development was American self-help author Napoleon Hill. He was passionate about self-discipline. He believed it was a key ingredient to personal growth and organising your life.

He said: *"Self-discipline begins with the mastery of your thoughts. If you don't control what you think, you can't control what you do. Simply, self-discipline enables you to think first and act afterwards."*

When you first read this quote, it makes perfect sense, but how many of us put this into practice in our lives?

Our lives are busy, but our thoughts don't need to be as well. Sometimes we can get lost along the way. If this resonates with you, then you are on the right track. Discipline can give you a clear direction. It can also remind you that nobody has to be perfect. You are on the first step to regaining control of your life and enjoying it the way you want to.

Discipline can bring order to the things that generally annoy you on an everyday basis. Research shows <u>self-discipline with emotional intelligence gives you a higher</u> chance of success. It can help you resist distractions, stay focused on your goals and be successful.

CONQUER DISCIPLINE WITH YOUR GUIDE

It can be easy for us to deep dive into subjects. Personal experience shows us unless we use the information we read, we will forget it. This book has an easy and effective system to make sure you remember. At the end of each chapter, you can put into action what you have learned before you move on to the next section.

This simple process allows you to incorporate it into your day with ease.

View it as your guidebook with actionable tips along the way.

- Learn about different habits and how you can create them to work for you.
- Use small daily rituals to start becoming more disciplined immediately.
- Change your mindset to help you feel empowered to try new things.
- Action easy lifestyle changes for yourself to gain personal freedom.
- Find out how to end distractions so you can stay laser-focused.
- Discover meditation and mindfulness methods to help you relax and clear your mind.

You can learn all the above and more. You can take ownership of your life and change it for the better. It does take time, but the rewards are so worth it. You will experience freedom from life-restricting thought patterns. Start practising gratitude and bring out the best in you. You will also notice a positive change in all your relationships. With all the people you love, with friends and with your colleagues.

Your mind needs to think in a different way to create something extraordinary.

Some of the strategies and tasks in the book will push you to your limits. You will do things you have never done before. Embrace it and see it through. There is no need to worry about it. Nothing can stop you when you have the right tools. Failures become opportunities and can motivate you further. You can achieve your dreams and enrich your life at the same time.

Mental discipline is achievable for anybody.

Chapter 1 is the beginning of your journey. By following the process, you will learn more about yourself. You will find that goal setting can be fun, and mental discipline practices can support you along the way. When you finish the book, you will be ready to progress further in your personal development. There is no limit to where you can go.

Get ready to begin your self-discovery journey. Learn the magical tools in each chapter to conquer discipline. Free your mind and create the best version of yourself. Let's get started!

1

WHAT IS DISCIPLINE? IS IT EVEN IMPORTANT?

"Self-discipline is what separates the winners and the losers."

— THOMAS PETERFFY

Think about the last time you set yourself a goal and failed. It's a horrible feeling when you work so hard to achieve something, but it all ends in a bad way. It might have knocked your confidence and self-esteem. Sometimes you can feel scared of giving it another go.

You need to know that those failures were not your fault.

There is no need to beat yourself up. People fail day after day, but the real winners keep going and don't let it deter them. You know those people who seem to be in the right place and at the right time. Luck does not come into it. They all use an internal power that keeps them compelled and driven to succeed.

Successful people use self-discipline to help them achieve their goals.

So, what is self-discipline? The dictionary definition tells us it is "the ability to make yourself do things you know you should do even when you do not want to."

The definition even implies that there has to be a drive from within you to succeed. It's not like turning on a tap and expecting a cascade of inner action to flow out of you. It's an inner ability that you can use to succeed in life. It doesn't matter what you want to achieve. You only need to use your discipline in the right way.

Sometimes the things we want the most in life might be hard to get, but they are not impossible. It means we need to use our mental prowess to achieve them. You don't need to be a specialist in anything. You can use an easy system that works like clockwork to help you succeed.

Self-discipline gives you a gentle push so you can keep jumping the hurdles in life.

You will already know some people who have achieved success. I can guarantee they didn't get there through sheer luck. Pretty much anybody successful has had to find their inner self-discipline to succeed. They use practical strategies and build good habits.

At the end of the day, it is a process you can tap into to help you be more effective. Everybody can use this skill to improve themselves. It doesn't matter who you are or your situation. It is an excellent tool for personal development novices. Or for anybody who wants to progress further in their personal development.

THE FLEXIBILITY OF DISCIPLINE

There is no denying it. Discipline might seem like a harsh, rigid word. Yet, it has a surprising amount of flexibility when you know how to use it. When problems or challenges arise, you can adjust and keep moving toward your goals. It can help you finish tasks instead of throwing in the towel. Some people might refer to it as:

- Endurance
- Restraint

- Perseverance

Whatever you want to call it, it is that inner ability to keep pushing through no matter what happens to you. You might have experienced distractions and temptations in your attempts for goal success. Sometimes you might have stopped sooner than you thought. When you do this, you usually settle for an alternative result. This decision is the second-best option. Luckily, you don't have to settle for second best situations any more.

If you stick to it like glue, it can help you to achieve your dreams and goals.

When you use self-discipline, it makes everything seem easier. You are not time-watching or searching for distractions. You are 100% focused on the task at hand. You can use it in all areas of your life. There are no hard-and-fast rules where you can use it. At times it might feel like you are only making "baby steps", but each step adds up to a giant leap towards your goal. Discipline is the true goal-slayer if you stick to your plan.

SHORTBREAD BISCUIT MASTERY

A perfect, fun example would be one of my sister's abilities to use self-discipline. It's her love of shortbread fingers. She knows she has a sweet tooth but can still control these sugary temptations. If you know shortbread, it is hard to stop once you start. It's so tasty. The great British tradition of having shortbread with a cup of tea is one of my family's favourites.

My sister has always controlled her shortbread intake since she was very young. She allows herself two shortbread fingers, and then she stops. She still does it today. It is fair to say she mastered the art of self-discipline a long time ago, and it has helped her stay trim as a result.

She doesn't feel she is "missing out," as she uses her inner strength to look after herself. She can eat an extra biscuit and love every single bit of it. The reason she doesn't eat another one is that she knows she will regret it later on. She uses self-discipline to handle the situation. Her discipline outweighs the temptation in front of her.

It's not only biscuits. I have never seen anybody in my entire life with as much discipline as my sister. She has used this ability in all areas of her life, including her career. Discipline has helped her travel with her work in education throughout the world. Once you start using it, the knock-on effect in your life can be incredible.

Discipline can help give you what you are always looking for - self-control.

This self-control is vital if you want to reach your goals. Once you can control yourself, you can use this ability to achieve whatever you want. It might sound incredible, but it is 100% possible for us all.

A SUPERPOWER AGAINST ENDLESS DISTRACTIONS

A Carleton study in 2017 discovered <u>we spend a third of our working time attending to emails.</u> With all this going on, it is normal to feel indecisive or lazy when you have so much to respond to. It wasn't like this 30 years ago, but it is now our reality every day of our lives.

There are so many things in the world that can influence us. You see constant images on the television, social media online, the latest trends, our family and friends.

There is a never-ending barrage of information for us to process. Information overload is a real modern-day problem.

When you use discipline to manage everything, you can lead a more moderate life. You also become more patient with yourself and others. You will find your life changes from "being busy" to one more organised.

It is a superpower, as it gives you more freedom in your life.

Once you start using this new power, you won't want to go back. You will feel more able to do things, as you know, you are in control of them. You are in control of your life. You are the driver and can control the accelerator pedal.

SELF-DISCIPLINE CAN ENRICH YOUR LIFE

So now you know what discipline is, how important is it to you?

Well, it is a must-have. It can be there holding your hand as you march on through every difficult challenge, test, and trial.

- It is your secret tool that can propel you forward every single day. Even on those days when you feel a little down, you can rely on it to keep you going.
- It can remind you of what you need to do and when to do it.
- It pushes you to keep going and not get bogged down in the details.

A paper published this year in the *Proceedings of the National Academy of Sciences* gave an insight into the long term effects of discipline. The researchers studied a group of children from birth to their mid-forties. It found children handled financial, health, and social demands better in later life.

This result proves that using discipline early in your life is great preparation. It is akin to preparing yourself for what is ahead, not only for your goals. You might be thinking you have "missed the boat" as you are no longer a child, but it is not the case. Anybody can start using self-discipline at any time in their lives.

You only need to be willing to give it a go and get started. You might have never heard about discipline at school, but it doesn't matter. You have already had important life lessons and experienced good and bad events. You know, deep down inside of you that there is an easier way to manage everything. This is it.

KEEPING YOUR EYE ON THE PRIZE

Without discipline, you can experience different forms of failure and loss. It can affect your health and your relationships. You can also start suffering from low confidence and self-esteem. You might even blame others for your failures, and so the cycle repeats itself.

It is so easy to give up at that first hurdle and "change your goal". You might decide your original goal was too hard and assume that is why you failed. Discipline can become one of the most important things in your life. It can end your struggle to complete goals.

Discipline breaks the false illusion of failure and keeps you going till you get there.

Instead of settling for a small promotion at work, you will become the main manager. You lose weight as you exercise and eat well, but you can keep going till you get to your main target goal. You do 3 hours per day of your online course like clockwork until completing it by your intended date. These are the types of things you can achieve.

THE VALUE OF DISCIPLINE

Anything worth pushing to have is always going to have value for you. Nobody expects to coast through life and receive everything on a silver platter. Sure, hard work is usually needed, especially if you start a business or project from scratch. The key to real success is to couple this effort with discipline. It's all about putting off short-term pleasures to wait and enjoy the long-term gains.

Serial entrepreneur, Richard Branson, said: *"Hard-won things are more valuable than those that come too easily."*

We spend so much of our lives searching for time to do the things we want to do. You only need a bit of guidance and a few easy organisational skills. You can create a self-discipline structure that will work for you. It might not feel like it when you are grinding out the hours to achieve your goal, but this book will show you how to do it.

You don't need to be Ariana Huffington, Elon Musk, or Richard Branson to master the art of self-discipline.

The chances are you already use some self-discipline and might not even realise it. The good news is there is so much more you can do. It is so valuable that you will be wondering why you didn't do it before. You don't need to be a pro athlete or business magnate to use it. Nothing is stopping you from using it for your benefit.

People are aware of self-discipline, but many don't know how it works. Pro athletes, for example, are only too familiar with this view. On the sports website, TriathlonLab, they state,

> *"people acknowledge the importance and benefits of self-discipline, but very few take real steps to develop and strengthen it."*

USING DISCIPLINE TO ACHIEVE SUCCESS

By now, you should realise how powerful discipline can be. It is key if you want to be successful in life and become the best version of yourself. You will still have bad days, but your new mental toughness will not recognise them as you keep pushing on. Temptations will always arise, as that is life, but how you handle them makes you successful. Your behaviour can make a huge difference in how it all works.

If you still need some convincing, think about this quote from the highly successful American football coach Lou Holtz: *"Without self-discipline, success is impossible, period."* It is a bold statement, but he has been there and done it. This progressive mentality is also possible for you. You don't need to have had a successful coaching career, only a willingness to be more disciplined.

Be honest with yourself and think back to all your successes and failures. You will see a connection to your failures. Your failures connect to one of these three things - 1) Giving up, 2) Looking for an easier solution, and 3) Procrastinating. Whereas in contrast, your successes so far in life have all had one thing in common - a huge amount of discipline.

Success in life can mean different things to everybody on our planet. Whatever success means to you, it is achievable. It is always a long-term commitment that yields fantastic results. Short-term goals might bring you some quick excitement. The long-term ones, though, are far more rewarding.

TRAITS OF SUCCESSFUL PEOPLE THAT USE DISCIPLINE

There are common characteristics of people that use discipline to achieve their success. Some of them are quite obvious, but others not as much. You might recognise some of these traits in yourself. Or realise they are there, but you have not been using them.

- People with strong discipline take the necessary action. They don't sit around talking about things. They do them.
- They pick goals they are passionate about. This process helps them to use their self-discipline and to keep going.
- Time management is essential to them, and they use time well.
- They understand the need to use long-term strategies to get what they want. Instead of looking for a "quick fix," they know it will take time.
- Discipline lovers are willing to cut ties with people and things that are holding them back. It might seem ruthless, but it gets results.
- A plan is there for a reason, and they stick to it without fail.
- Challenges excite them, and they like completing complicated tasks. It makes them feel satisfied and ready to jump over the next hurdle.

THE REAL BENEFITS OF DISCIPLINE

The main aim is to be successful in achieving your goals. There will also be many other noticeable changes in your life. It's not only about reaching goals. It is a positive momentum with real change. Here are some of the benefits you will notice:

- You start creating habits that lead you to be more disciplined in life.
- You achieve things, as you are now completing things instead of giving up.
- You are more focused and less prone to distractions and procrastination.
- You become a master. Whatever your success is, you become a master in it.
- Your confidence improves, and you have fewer moments of self-doubt.
- Your work and life quality improve as you are successful.
- You become the best version of yourself.

CHAPTER ONE - ACTION STEP

By following the Action Steps at the end of each chapter, you can progress and master the art of discipline. It is best not to move on to the next chapter until you feel satisfied that you have completed this Action Step.

You should now have a better understanding of what discipline is and how it can help you achieve your goals.

I am sure that you feel excited about learning more about discipline and how it can improve your life.

Before you proceed to the next chapter, it is time for you to take your first action step.

- Write down what you would like to achieve. It can be one or several goals, whatever you prefer. You can type on your mobile, tablet or PC so you can edit it till it feels right. Unless you are old-fashioned like me, you can use pen and paper to write it down, old school style. (Sometimes, writing things down can be more reflective as it slows the process, so you think as you write).
- Now visualise in your mind the success of these goals. Think about how it will make you feel? It would help if you started experiencing that feeling now instead of waiting for it.
- Next, you need to break down the goal or goals into workable sections. Think about the individual things you need to do to achieve the goals you have set yourself. Also, make a note of these, so everything is clear.

The rest of this book will help you to achieve these goals. If you read the chapters and follow the action steps, you can instil discipline in your life. This process will help you to achieve your personal and professional goals.

2

MOTIVATION - NO THANKS, I'M DANDY

"Motivation gets you going, but discipline keeps you growing."

— JOHN C. MAXWELL

In the last chapter, we learnt what discipline is and how it is important in your lives. So you might be wondering if using motivation is the same thing. It's the word that pops up in most personal development books. Motivation is the subject we should look at to develop ourselves, right? Well, this chapter will help you understand why that is not the case. Discipline is the real winner over motivation.

THE TWO TYPES OF MOTIVATION

Before we compare the two, it is useful to understand how motivation works. Psychologists refer to two different types of motivation - <u>extrinsic and intrinsic</u>. These two types of motivation explain our general everyday behaviour towards goals. Extrinsic motivation is about things from outside of us. Intrinsic motivation is anything that comes from inside us.

EXTRINSIC MOTIVATION

Extrinsic is when you use activity or behaviour to avoid punishment or earn a reward. The important point to note here is that we are not doing it for excitement. It is only reward-driven behaviour. We are doing it because we are trying to earn something or avoid something negative.

Here are some examples of extrinsic motivation:

- Hitting targets at work to receive a bonus
- Competing in sports to win trophies
- Losing weight, so you look better in your clothes
- Carrying out work to receive money
- Helping people to earn praise from people who know you

- Turning up to work on time to avoid problems with your manager
- Doing things for public attention or fame
- Buy one, get one free sale (BOGOF) offers

The downside of extrinsic motivation is you don't know what to do after you have received the reward. The value wears off over time.

INTRINSIC MOTIVATION

Intrinsic motivation is doing activities or behaviour because they resonate deep inside us. It is the internal interests and values we have as a person. This positive and interesting behaviour inside of us compels us to take action. We don't expect any reward for doing these things, as it is something very personal.

Here are some examples of intrinsic motivation:

- Challenging yourself to solve puzzles because you enjoy it
- Selecting healthy meals to eat as you love cooking them
- Taking time to exercise in the morning to feel good
- Learning about personal development because you want to improve yourself

- Helping others and not expecting anything in return
- Learning a new language to help you experience different cultures
- Engaging in creative activities, like reading and painting that relax you
- Play team sports to have fun and engage with others

A study at Cornell University in 2018 also found that immediate rewards can increase intrinsic motivation by strengthening the activity-goal association.

Intrinsic motivation is very personal and exciting. The downside is that it is difficult to stay motivated for goals on a long-term basis.

WHY MOTIVATION CAN BE A WOLF IN SHEEP'S CLOTHING

Because we are familiar with the term motivation, we think it is the main way to achieve goals. Motivation can help you as you work towards your goals, but discipline is stricter. You can regard motivation as a short term tool. It's not designed for long-term ventures. You need to understand the clear differences between discipline and motivation to succeed.

Motivation is a fleeting emotion, it comes, and it goes.

The main benefit of motivation is that it's like nitrous oxide running through your blood. It gives you the oomph to take action. This feels great, but it's a fleeting emotion. The feeling will disappear at some point. Usually, after a few days, and that's if you're lucky.

Discipline, in contrast, is not an emotion.

When discipline comes into the equation, motivation pales in comparison. There are no highs and lows like you get with motivation. It's like having an invisible drill instructor who keeps pushing you forward. Emotion is never a factor in play here. You know what you have to do, and you need to keep going. No questions asked. You follow the plan and keep going. It's as simple as that.

Because we hear and see the term motivation quite often in our lives, we assume motivation is the only way. In comparison, discipline doesn't get as much press as motivation does, but it should.

MOTIVATION VERSUS DISCIPLINE

You need to understand the clear differences between discipline and motivation. This understanding will help you to succeed and achieve your goals. Using a combination of both can help you get there, but discipline can keep you on track for the long-term.

Discipline has stamina, longevity and gives you control. Motivation does work, but it is so temporary in comparison. Motivation can create enthusiasm and excitement for a project. This can be helpful, especially if you are prone to procrastination.

The excitement makes everything positive and propels you. Sometimes, you might finish projects quicker in the excitement of it all. This is the pure adrenaline rush. This is how motivation gets great PR. But the buzz doesn't last.

An Example Of Motivation Failure vs Discipline

Exercising is a great example of how it can all go wrong. Think about a new exercise routine that you started, but you ended up stopping. This might have happened several times in your life. When you look back, you might recognise a continual pattern. You had the excitement in the beginning, but as time went on, the novelty wore off.

What went wrong? It wasn't you.

It was that pesky devil called motivation that ran out of steam. You lost your emotional attachment to the task. Here are some common excuses to stop exercise:

- It was too cold in the morning/or the night.
- You think you have a slight sniffle and are not feeling well.
- You were feeling sore from the last lot of exercise, so you needed to rest.
- You've done it a few days this week already. That will be enough.

- You want to have a lay-in because you want more sleep.
- It's the weekend so you can have a break.

These are a few of the excuses that people use to sneak out of exercising. Then, before you know it, your exercise routine has failed, and you are back to square one. In this example, if you had used discipline, you could have handled these excuses and ignored them. Your inner self-discipline would make you go out and do the exercise without fail. You would wrap up warm and get out there, sniffle or not.

Discipline is the star that shines bright and leads you to success.

Remember the definition of discipline? It's all about doing something good for you, even when you don't want to. It is all about being consistent and showing up, even when you want to stay in bed and sleep. If you use discipline, you can gain yourself freedom from the emotion of motivation.

This quote is from one of the greatest minds, and he attributes his success to self-discipline.

"I could only achieve success in my life through self-discipline, and I applied it until my wish and my will became one."

— NIKOLA TESLA

Tesla completely believed in the power of self-discipline for his success in life.

In his quote, he even touches on the effort required to get there. He wished for it, and it happened because he applied self-discipline. Note that he makes no mention of motivation.

DISCIPLINE IS THE MASTER - MOTIVATION IS THE PUPIL

Discipline and motivation are important, but discipline would win the battle if they fought it out. A study in secondary schools in Kenya in 2017 looked for strategies to improve students' self-motivation. The study found that promoting self-discipline was key to improving self-motivation.

The Kenyan study detailed *"self-discipline is the capacity to control one's thoughts, speech and deeds to attain the desired achievement."* In a nutshell, this section explains how discipline can help us to achieve what we desire.

Ultimately, discipline keeps you going when you run out of motivation. It can drive you to complete tasks and even ones that you don't like. This is because you know that it is a long-term strategy that will work for you. You might have high intrinsic motivation. This is the same that athletes use, but like them, you still need self-discipline to succeed.

WHAT ABOUT WILLPOWER? WHAT IS IT?

Willpower is also another tool that you can use for your personal development. The dictionary definition tells us that "willpower is the ability to control your own thoughts and the way in which you behave". You might think willpower is the same as motivation, but they are different. Willpower has a connection to thinking and understanding what action you are going to do. In comparison, motivation is all about the connection with your emotions.

THE CONNECTION BETWEEN SELF-CONTROL AND WILLPOWER

When you look at how willpower works with discipline. That's when it starts getting interesting. The main differences are the duration of its effect and the intensity. You can look upon willpower as a burst of thinking energy at a certain moment in time.

Willpower helps you do the right thing in that particular moment. In contrast, self-discipline is more thought out. It is a long-term process instead of a quick reaction.

The Chocolate and Radish Experiment

There have been many studies to determine the connection between self-control and willpower. The three main trains of thoughts about self-control and willpower were:

1. The mind processes information and works out what it has to do, and then does it.
2. Willpower is like energy or strength from within.
3. That it is a skill, you can learn as a child and onwards.

The experiment that managed to get the answer was the *Chocolate and Radish experiment.* It was conducted in 1996 by Roy Baumeister and his colleagues at Case Western Reserve University. The findings were published in 1998.

Who would have thought that chocolates and radishes would go in the same sentence? But it was a 100% legit experiment that has been classed as groundbreaking research in self-control. The participants had to face a food challenge designed to deplete their willpower by unfilling a promise of chocolate.

The Details Of The Experiment

- The first part of the research consisted of 67 participants placed in a room that smelt of lovely freshly baked chocolate cookies.
- The participants were then shown the cookies as well as other chocolate goods.
- Some were able to eat the chocolate goods. The other participants that were in the experimental control had to eat radishes instead.

As you can imagine, the radish eaters were not best pleased. Apparently, some of them even went and picked up the cookies to smell them.

Once the scientists finished the *food-bait and switch* part of the research. They gave the participants a second exercise that was meant to be unrelated to the first one. It was a *persistence-testing puzzle,* and the results were incredible.

- The radish eaters made less attempts and spent half the time trying to solve the puzzle than the chocolate eaters.
- This showed that the radish eaters could not find the willpower to try to complete the puzzle. They were too tired to give it a go.

The Three Predicted Results

The scientists, before the experiment, considered the three different areas and predicted the following results for each theory:

1. The information processing theory assumed that the participants would do better on the second task because their self-control module would be active from the first task.
2. The second theory assumed you would do worse on the second task as your strength or energy (willpower) would be depleted from the first task.
3. The last theory predicted there would be no change as a skill takes time to develop over many occasions.

GROUNDBREAKING RESULTS THAT SHATTERED OLD THEORIES

The experiment was a breakthrough for psychologists. It proved when people used self-control in different tasks that willpower could deplete. It was like comparing it to a muscle that would get tired after using it. So it would not be effective in the short-term.

The Chocolate and Radish experiment became a foundational study. It helped birth hundreds of other studies on the subject.

The experiment results showed that the old theories of cognitive process and information processing models were not right.

Ego Depletion

Baumeister and his colleagues were also shocked by the results. They knew that they would not be popular in the psychological community. It was the first time that scientists had put forward a theory based on energy. Baumeister called the theory "Ego Depletion".

He based the name on Freud's work. Freud was the last theorist that said humans were energy and worked by energy processes. Ego depletion is the idea that self-control and willpower take from a limited mental resource pool.

You can see ego depletion when people tire at the end of the day. They give in to temptations when their willpower and self-control are low.

Further Discoveries About Willpower

Since the initial experiment, scientists have discovered that willpower depletes in other ways, not only by self-control.

- When you make choices and decisions.
- If you use your initiative.

- Planning and executing plans.

Psychologists found that people are subject to ego depletion in their everyday lives. People don't even need manipulation in an experiment to have their willpower zapped.

They discovered that there is a connection between the body's basic energy supply. When glucose spreads around the bloodstream, it is like "brain fuel", as it provides energy for activities in the brain. Also, neurotransmitters consist of glucose.

Baumeister made some more food challenge exercises to test his theory on glucose. His team found that when participants had ice-cream to eat. They then went on to show an improvement in self-control in a second task. They did the same experiment on a control group with boring, unappetising food. This group still managed to improve their self-control.

This led them to discover that willpower has a connection to glucose in the body. They found that blood glucose levels dropped in people who had exerted self-control. When they gave them a dose of glucose, it counteracted the effects of go depletion. There is also a train of thought that this is why some women may struggle with PMS. It is because the glucose is low in the body, and this can affect their self-control.

All these discoveries give more credence to the body and mind connection. Later chapters will look at this in more detail.

CREATING HABITS AS AN ALTERNATIVE

Ego depletion has been a controversial subject in the last few years. So far, there have been over 600 studies that have confirmed its existence. Yet, the battle continues in the psychological community. Luckily, there is an alternative to consider and one that works. One that would drop the need for willpower and all its connotations.

It is the creation of habits.

Creating habits that reinforce a positive mindset. It can give you even greater power and focus on achieving success. We will go into more detail about habits later in the book. Don't forget that your self-discipline should be the main focus for you. It is also good to remember that motivation and willpower do have their parts to play. You can use all three, with an emphasis on disciplining yourself.

The next time somebody offers you a chocolate bar when you are on a diet, you will notice certain things. You can enjoy your personal development journey at different levels. Your willpower will stop you from accepting it at that moment, as you know it will mess up your plans. Discipline will stop you from eating chocolate every single day. Plus, when you bring habits into the equation, your development will skyrocket.

CHAPTER TWO - ACTION STEP

You have learnt about the differences between discipline, motivation, and willpower. Your understanding of these areas is a key indicator of how successful you will be. Motivation and willpower are useful tools. Using self-discipline with habits will ensure that you reach your goals.

This is your second action step in the book. Put some quiet time aside so you can complete it with a clear mind.

- It is time to start thinking about the habits that will help you maintain your goals.
- It can also help to start visualising your end goal/goals. Imagine how you will feel when you have achieved your goal/goals. This can help

you to determine the habits you need to get there.
- Look back at the goal/goals you set yourself at the end of Chapter One. Write down three habits that you can start now.
- Start the habits from tomorrow and make a note every time you use one of them. This process will help you see how often you use them and at what moment. It will also give you a head start before we get to the habit section of the book.

Once you are happy that you have completed this action step, please move on to the next chapter.

3

WHAT GOES IN MUST COME OUT

"Self-discipline is self-caring."

— M. SCOTT PECK

By now, you realise that you can use discipline in all areas of your life. It's more than setting some goals and using discipline to reach them. Your health is also a key ingredient on this road to success. If you want to succeed in life, you need to feel good.

How do you expect to be the best version of yourself unless you treat your body well?

Exactly, as the heading of this chapter says, what goes in must come out. If you fill your body with rubbish, it can affect you physically. This principle also applies to your mental health. If you are reading and watching negative things, it will be a drain on your positive mindset. It only makes sense that positive actions will come out of you if you feel healthy and positive inside.

By taking the time to give yourself "self-care," you can give yourself a clear head start in your life goals.

Your physical and mental health are both essential. So I decided to create separate chapters to cover both of them. This chapter will focus on the physical aspects of health. The next chapter will cover areas to help your mental health. We can then move on to the power of creating everyday habits.

WHAT DOES YOUR HEALTHY MINDSET LOOK LIKE?

When it comes to health, eating healthy and exercising regularly spring to mind. Richard Branson, as a successful entrepreneur, understands the importance of a healthy mindset. In his blog, he states, *"I make sure I find at least 60 minutes a day to focus on my health."* This recipe for a healthy lifestyle might seem straightforward, but sometimes we can make things difficult for ourselves. There are so many daily temptations that can sway you from making a healthy choice.

Eating a pizza, watching Netflix, and drinking coke. It sometimes feels more rewarding at the end of a hard day than a salad and a power walk.

It is your bad lifestyle choices that can create poor health. We always know what we have to do, but it can be hard to feel motivated to do them. But by nurturing yourself and making healthy choices. You can remove tired choices and turn things around.

It won't happen overnight. But, as we know, with discipline, long-term goals can be far more rewarding if we stick with them. Discipline is inside us all. We need to practice it and develop it as a skill. As they say, practice makes perfect, and so does discipline.

Start viewing discipline as an inner strength you own. Not the harsh word people associate with it.

There is nothing to stop you from activating your discipline right now. It helps you make the right decisions. Using discipline can give you more control over your daily actions and reactions.

The Benefits Of Using Discipline For Your Body

When you start using even a small amount of discipline, the changes can be impressive. Here are some examples of how you can start incorporating discipline into your life:

- It stops you from eating unhealthy food. You can use your inner strength to stop ordering a takeaway and make a fresh, healthy meal instead.
- You can reduce the amount of food you eat and check your food portions.
- It can help you reduce the amount of alcohol that you drink. This will stop your drinking from becoming a bad habit.
- Drug use, including smoking, has a connection to discipline. Your self-discipline can help you see the benefits of not being "high".
- Using a little bit of discipline can get you off the sofa and out for a walk. You can start exercising more and see and feel the effects on your body.
- If you want to lose weight, using discipline can keep you going to achieve your target weight loss.

According to a statistic in 2020 from the World Health Organization (WHO), obesity in the world has nearly tripled since 1975. With a statistic such as that, there is clear and present danger in the world of obesity in the world. This can have effects on individuals, their families, and healthcare throughout the world.

While many countries have already stated health campaigns to address these issues. There is still a lot of work needed to help stop this trend. You can separate people into three groups when it comes to their health choices:

1. People who always eat well and exercise.
2. Those people who eat well and exercise for a time. Stop. Then start again.
3. People who eat rubbish and don't like to exercise.

By using discipline, we can stay more in group 1. It would be hard to stay in group 1 unless we were an athlete. While we are in group 1, we may have a treat. After all, a little treat now and then doesn't hurt anybody. You could also use a treat as a reward when you reach a specific mini-target in your health goals.

Which group do you currently fit into?

If you are currently in group 3, don't despair. There can be many reasons why you are there. Here are a few of them:

- You might have a busy schedule that forces you to make the wrong food choices.
- You suffer from ego depletion (as discussed in the previous chapter). You are too tired to exercise or eat well at the end of the day.
- The food you eat is bad for you, but very tasty, and you don't want to change it.
- You don't have intrinsic or extrinsic motivation to exercise.
- You think you can't afford to exercise or eat healthy, so you don't bother.

I was in group 3 and decided to move to group 1. It took me time, and it wasn't easy, but I managed to do it. I also visualised how I would look and feel when I reached my goal. This visualisation process helped me to keep focus and stay on track.

I was able to lose 30lbs and increase my confidence tenfold. I also became a better leader in my personal and working life as a result.

When you feel good, you do good in your life. Everything changes for the better. The knock-on effect on my personal and professional life was incredible. I started to excel at work, and my relationships with my family and loved ones were deeper and happier. I had an abundance of energy, and my mindset was more positive.

If I can do it, so can you. It always takes that first step to get going, but it can help to give you freedom in your life. You don't have to be a slave to your food and exercise demons that encourage you to eat wrong and be lazy. You can decide to pick the healthier, happier option and start changing your life for the better.

DON'T JUDGE A BOOK BY ITS COVER

When it comes to health, we sometimes have ideas about what a healthy, fit body should look like. We see images in magazines of perfect models. But, everybody is different, and so are our bodies.

A good example would be my sister-in-law's recent health experience. A doctor told my sister-in-law that she has high cholesterol. This was quite surprising. For those of use who might remember the cartoon Popeye, she resembles more Olive than Bluto.

I mention this story as many people associate overweight people with bad diets. This is not true. I spoke to my sister in law about this, who was getting mocked by her siblings. I wanted to get to the bottom of it, as there was more than met the eye.

She confessed to me that she has an unhealthy obsession with cheese. She was eating cheese with every meal.

I'm no doctor, but I think the cheese was a contributing factor for her high cholesterol level. It is a fine example of how things might not be as they seem. On a more serious note, it also demonstrates how important it is to stay healthy and on top of your health in general. So, even if you are in group 3 above, it might be wise to rethink your health, as I did.

CHANGE YOUR OUTLOOK AND HELP YOUR BODY

Like Oscar Wilde said, *"I can resist anything except temptation."* Suppose you love cheese like my sister-in-law. You can probably relate to this quote and how she feels. It doesn't have to be a cheese obsession. It can be a sugar craving, and you end up having two sugars with your coffee every day. Or you love chocolate and keep buying it for a treat, but it gets out of hand.

Changing your outlook on how you view healthy habits can be a game-changer.

You don't need to view exercise and dieting as chores. You can put an element of fun into them. This change will make it seem easier and not as challenging. Also, as soon as you exercise more and eat better, there are other knock-on effects on your health.

Discipline can be far-reaching in your life. You can sleep better at night and get the sleep that your body needs to rejuvenate itself. This, in turn, encourages your personal standards to improve. You wake up on time, feel refreshed and don't miss appointments.

Also, as your body becomes fitter and loses weight, you gain more energy, helping you in other areas of your life. Not to mention the positive vibes that you emanate. These vibes can attract other positive things and opportunities.

THE INVISIBLE THREAT

It's also worth remembering that health problems with the body are not always visible. Cardiovascular diseases, diabetes, hypertension, and stress, can all be silent killers.

You only need to look at the [recent studies of the global burden of diabetes](#) to see there is a worrying trend. Like my sister-in-law, you might look like a picture of health but on the inside, it can be a different story altogether.

Whatever it is that pushes your "naughty but nice" button, you can make a quick change now. It can help you in the long-term.

- Remove the temptation and put it where you can't see it. Hide the cheese or other tempting item or get somebody to do it for you.
- Cut your sugar consumption. Go from two teaspoons to one.
- Walk a different way around the supermarket, so you don't see the chocolate aisle.

As you can see above, they are not major changes. But, they can end up having a big impact on your life. It is possible if you can commit to it and visualise the result. Imagine being a happier and healthier version of yourself. You can use your discipline to stick to it and enjoy the results.

IT'S ALL ABOUT GOOD VIBRATIONS

You can also make the right choices when it comes to selecting the food you eat. We all know it is great to eat salad and vegetables. But, there are so many diets flying around at a time. It can be hard to know which one is best for you.

I personally believe that everybody has a diet and fitness regime that works best for them.

So you may need to try a few out before you find the one that matches your body type and lifestyle. Don't be despondent if it doesn't work at first. Keep going until you find that system that ticks all your boxes and makes you feel good.

An interesting concept is eating food that has good vibrations. As we discovered in the last chapter, scientists confirmed Freud's theories on energy. But it is not only humans that have energy. There is a train of thought that everything around us has some form of energy, including our food.

This might seem a strange concept, but it's not all mumbo jumbo.

The science of nutrition is based heavily on food content, especially concerning its chemical side. Nutritionists have found that food is better for our body if it has the right minerals and vitamins.

A fundamental concept in physics has shown that every living thing and food item has energy in it.

Scientists, including the famous French engineer, André Simoneton, researched this energy to determine which food was good and bad for the body.

Researching Vibrational Energy

The first step was to measure the body's energy by using a counter that measured radiation. Because bodies emit radiation, scientists can measure it in colour and sound. The vibrational range for a human body is normally 6,200 - 7,000 angstroms.

A person who is in good health should have a vibration of at least 6,500 angstroms. It was discovered that anybody who had a lower value than this had diseases or incorrect food attitudes.

The main thing to note here is that environmental radiation can affect human nutrition.

Sadly, this environmental radiation can affect our bodies. It can affect the vibrations of everything, which in turn can affect our health. Just as we absorb into our bodies the minerals and vitamins that our body needs, we can also absorb their vibrations.

Experiments have shown that we can eat healthy food with the right nutrients but that the positive vibrational energy has been cancelled out. Modified food and synthetic food are good examples of this in action.

This vibrational change in the food is negative for us and does not help us with optimum development or healthy ageing.

Simoneton used vibrational food to heal himself when he was gravely ill. When he found out that there was no hope for his recovery, he set out to find a way to heal himself. He was already an expert in electromagnetism, and through the 1930s and 1940s, he collaborated with research into vibrational food. He was able to regain his health by changing his diet to vegetarianism.

THE FOUR CATEGORIES OF VIBRATIONAL FOOD

Food has calories or chemical energy, but Simoneton also recorded the electromagnetic power or vibrational power of food. He discovered that people must try to keep their vibration around 6,500 angstroms. He divided food into four general categories.

Category One (6,500 angstroms - 10,000 angstroms)

- Mature fruits and fruit juices (squeezed).
- Raw, fresh vegetables and fruit cooked below 70 degrees.
- Bread, cereals and flour only with whole grains.
- Olive oil.
- Sweet almonds, sunflower seeds, coconut, soy, hazelnuts, and peanuts.

Category One food is of the highest quality. It is important to mention that some food was superior when consumed shortly after production, such as:

- Butter
- Eggs
- Milk
- Fermented cheese
- Olive Oil
- Sea fish
- Shellfish

Category Two (3,000 angstroms - 6,500 angstroms)

- Vegetables that have been cooked in boiled water
- Milk
- Fridge butter
- Eggs that have not been freshly laid
- Honey
- Cooked Fish
- Sugar cane
- Wine
- Peanut oil

Category Three (Below 3,000 angstroms)

This category includes items with weak vibrational energy.

- Cooked meats
- Coffee
- Tea
- Chocolate
- Jams
- Processed cheese
- White bread

Category Four (No energy or angstroms)

- Margarine
- Alcoholic spirits

- Refined white sugar
- Bleached flour

THE POWER OF VEGETABLES

The research by Simoneton supports people who believe a vegetarian diet consisting of fresh vegetables and whole grains has the strongest life force and energy. Vegetables are at their most radiant when they come from the garden. They lose a third of their strength once they arrive at the supermarkets and another third after they are cooked.

Apparently, potatoes are powerhouses, which become stronger after they are cooked. The potato measures 2,000 when raw, but when it is boiled it is 7,000, and 9,000 when it is baked. Legumes, such as beans, lentils and peas, measure anything from 7,000 to 8,000 when they are fresh.

THE EFFECTS OF FOOD PROCESSING

Simoneton found in his research that food processing is extremely detrimental to the quality of food. For example, milk has a value of 6,500 angstroms when it is fresh, but within 24 hours, it loses 90% of its potency. After pasteurisation, there are no angstroms recorded.

These conclusions are also backed up by recommendations from scriptures and texts from different religions. Also, interestingly, the healing waters of Lourdes measure as high as 14,000 angstroms. That is certainly food for thought.

SETTING REALISTIC HEALTH GOALS

It's not only the food you eat that you need to consider. Goal setting is also an area that needs to be given a serious thought. It can sometimes be stressful when you are thinking about setting health goals. Because it is so personal, you can feel under pressure to set hardcore goals. These goals are not recommended as you are already subjecting your self-discipline to hard work right from the beginning.

It is more advisable to create health goals that are realistic and achievable. It doesn't matter if you walk for 10 minutes, and you feel shattered. Or if you lose 1lb in weight in a week when you wanted to lose more. You only have to keep going on your personal development journey.

Anything is better than doing nothing.

It is a process, and so is discipline. It is similar to using a muscle that becomes better and stronger over time. If it makes it easier for you, you can visualise seeing a disciplined muscle inside of you. You can see it flex and move as you use it in challenging situations. Or at the end of the night, see it in your mind's eye and see how much stronger the muscle is, and so are you.

Over time you will hit your goals and targets, and you will keep going.

Not because you feel forced, but because you are enjoying it and you have amazing results. Your blood tests will show everything is fine internally. Also, you will look and feel more fit and healthy externally. When you start getting the real results, it will motivate you to continue, and you can use your discipline to keep you going.

CHAPTER THREE - ACTION STEP

In this chapter, we have discussed the health of our bodies. You now know how influential a positive, healthy body can be. You have also learnt about different types of vibrational food that can help you with your discipline journey.

This is your third action step. Remember to schedule some time for yourself so that you can complete the action step without any distractions.

- Get ready to make a life-changing decision. What one better health choice will you make today? Write it down and place it somewhere; so you can see it every day.
- Commit to drinking more water every day. Aim for at least 2 litres.
- Take a daily walk and listen to something positive for 20 minutes.

In the next chapter, we will continue our health section by looking at our mental health and the body/mind connection.

4

FREE AS A BIRD

"Rule your mind or it will rule you."

— HORACE

In a world where mental issues are becoming more recognised. Learning how to clear our mind of negative thoughts can help us gain more freedom in life. Sometimes our thoughts can be our own worst enemy. Our imagination can run wild, and we end up creating negative, time-wasting stories.

If you want to be firing 100% on all cylinders, you need to feel your best, both mentally and physically.

When we let negative thoughts run rampant, it can affect our overall direction in life. Anything we can do to protect our minds from these unnecessary thoughts is worth it. It doesn't mean you are selfish when you decide to take a time-out. Self-care is essential. You can learn to fly like a free bird instead of feeling trapped inside your head prison.

This chapter will look at the different tools you can use to instil discipline into your mind. It will open your mind to the possibility of real change and how a few simple techniques can benefit you mentally. It will also help you cement the connection between your body and mind, so you are ready to start creating your new habits.

RESPECTING YOURSELF AND YOUR MENTAL HEALTH

The WHO released an article on World Mental Health Day in 2020. Two stark statistics made the headlines. The first was that <u>1 billion people globally were living with a mental disorder.</u> The second was that one person dies globally every 40 seconds from suicide.

These figures are scary and do make you sit up and take notice. But still, most countries only spend 2% of their health budgets on mental health. There is still lots of work to be done to support people mentally. But at last, people are now becoming more educated about the importance of protecting their mental health.

While mental conditions like anxiety, depression and bipolar disorder, to name only a few, are now more recognised. It will take time for the support to match the demand. It only makes sense that you should take some steps to look after yourself. A proactive approach to your mental health is far better than a reactive one when it may be too late.

We can become so fixated on our physical health that we forget about our mental health.

Our fast-paced lives are different from the ones our grandparents had. We are always trying to adjust to this fast pace and stay mentally fit. Some of us end up trying to do too much to fit it all in. This is not the answer, as it can lead to burnout. A more realistic and healthier approach is to take yourself out of this fast pace. You need to schedule some downtime so your brain can properly relax.

As mentioned earlier, it is not a selfish act to want to look after your mental health. After all, it is the same as going to the gym or going for a walk for your body. Except for this time, you are giving your mind space and exercises. It needs to reset itself. This process can help you to come back with more energy and mental prowess.

DIGGING YOURSELF OUT OF BAD SITUATIONS

In my teens, I was lucky enough to start a fantastic job in a bank. I was earning more money than my peers, and I admit to flashing the cash. However, I also learnt how easy it was to get credit from a bank. This led me to end up in serious financial debt. I remember feeling so depressed and low, with a mountain of debt and guilt.

I wondered how I would ever dig myself out of the hole I had put myself in.

My family circumstances changed in my late teens/the early twenties. I ended up being the main breadwinner for my family. My father was unable to work due to ill health, and my mother was busy looking after seven children. This forced me to confront my situation. I realised I had to take action to sort my finances out and look after my family. I dug deep and used my self-discipline to save myself.

At the time, I didn't even know I was using my inner discipline to help myself. However, looking back this was exactly what I had done. Discipline had saved me from a terrible situation and improved my life. I am eternally grateful for that experience, and from that moment on, I have always used discipline in my life. Admittedly, better in some areas of my life than others but it's important to remember personal development is a lifelong journey.

You see, it doesn't matter what situation you are in. There is always light at the end of the tunnel if you keep walking through the tunnel. You need to activate your inner strength and use your self-discipline. It can help you to turn any mentally stressful situation into a healthier one. It will help you create that better version of yourself. It might not happen overnight, but you will get there.

ELIMINATING MENTAL STRESS FROM GOAL-SETTING

Setting goals and creating habits should be fun. It shouldn't be seen as a tortuous test you have set yourself. It is your chance to achieve something you want and can develop yourself at the same time. Nobody feels inspired to work towards a goal when they feel stressed out.

Go gentle on yourself as you work towards your goals.

Cutting out the negative self-talk in your head can help you get there. Stay focused, and disciplined. If extra work or requests appear and you feel stressed, it is fine to say no. Nobody will think any less of you if you do. You are just preparing yourself to succeed and not fail again. You are protecting yourself and your mind from unnecessary stress.

As Heschel said,

"Self-respect is the fruit of discipline; the sense of dignity grows with the ability to say no to oneself."

— ABRAHAM JOSHUA HESCHEL

Another way of managing your goals is to <u>use journaling techniques to write down your progress</u>. Sometimes writing down your inner thoughts instead of keeping them in your head can help you feel less stressed. It can keep your mind clear and disciplined on working towards your goal.

You can also use other techniques to keep your head clear and keep those positive vibes flowing. Meditation, mindfulness, and practising gratitude can all help you to free your mind. Once again, you don't need to have any special prior training, only a willingness to give it a go.

MEDITATION CAN HELP TO BUILD YOUR SELF-DISCIPLINE

Meditation has had a resurgence in recent years. The notion of it being only for "hippies" and new-age practices kept it separate from mainstream society. Thankfully, it is more accepted, and people from all walks of life are enjoying the mental benefits of meditation. Even the army in America has decided to use meditation and yoga in a pilot programme for recruits. The aim is to see if it can help with mental toughness and stress management.

Meditation can help you lead a more fulfilling life. It can help to reduce your stress levels. But there are many other mental benefits from meditating:

- It can help ease tension headaches.
- It helps you have a better quality of sleep.
- Early research shows it can reduce memory loss as you age.
- It can improve your mental discipline and increase your self-awareness.

Meditation Is Easier Than You Think

You only need to do a few minutes each day. Afterwards, you will feel calm and relaxed. You might receive a sudden idea as your head is clear of information overload. Over time you can increase the time frame as you feel.

Meditating is a practice you can easily fit into your schedule.

Here is how to start using it in your life:

- Find a quiet area to relax and where you are comfortable.
- Listen to your breathing and focus on one thing, such as a candle.
- Clear your thoughts and relax.
- Every time a thought appears, flick it out of your mind.

You might receive a sudden idea as your head is clear of information overload. It is an easy way to centre yourself and control the thousands of thoughts running through your head.

Try Urge Surfing Your Negative Thoughts Away

We all love to watch people surfing. It's the anticipation of them finding the perfect wave and riding it out to the end. Well, you can get in on the action and try out some urge surfing. It is another form of meditating. It can help you manage your "weak-sauce" thoughts and make your thoughts stronger, so you can live in a "higher thought castle".

Imagine your thoughts are like waves and do some urge surfing.

The next time you meditate, imagine each thought is like a wave. When each thought comes, observe it inside your mind and don't be judgemental. Monitor these type of thoughts:

- "I need to eat that chocolate right now" - **Cravings**
- "I don't have to do that now, I can do it another time" - **Procrastination**
- "Go on, you can give in, one more time won't hurt" - **Urges**

These "weak-sauce" thoughts come and go, just like waves do. No wave is more important than another one. When each negative, weak wave comes, let it rise in your mind (surface), peak (reach its height) and then go down (crash on the beach).

As these thoughts crash on the beach, you can erase them from your mind. They are worthless thoughts that are now gone.

Every time you do this, you can build a positive "mindful" brick in your brain.

You will not entertain those same thoughts any more as they have crashed on the beach and have gone. With practice, you can live in your "higher thought" castle. Your discipline will make sure your "I give up/in" thoughts can't break through your mindful walls.

DEVELOPING YOUR DISCIPLINE FURTHER WITH MINDFULNESS

Now that you can see the value of using meditation, they are many mindfulness practices that can further develop your self-discipline. Mindfulness is a form of mediation when you focus on what you sense and feel in a particular moment.

You have no judgement on what you experience and feel. It is very focused and can also help to alleviate stress and clear your thoughts. It can be fantastic in a stressful situation as it transforms how you relate to experiences and events.

Instead of reacting negatively by feeling anxious or stressed, you can process things more positively.

You can also use mindfulness in more structured exercises instead of solely dealing with immediate situations. A couple of examples would be doing a Body Scan Meditation or a Walking Meditation.

Body Scan Meditation

Lie on your back with your legs laid flat. You can place your arms at your side, with the palms facing the ceiling. Slowly, focus your attention and scan every part of your body. Notice the emotions, feelings, or sensations that correspond to each area of the body.

Walking Meditation

Go somewhere quiet, where you have space in length from 3m to 6m. Start walking. Focus on the feeling as you walk the length and how your body keeps you upright and keeps your balance as you walk. Also, as you turn and walk back the other way, notice the sensations as you turn.

USING DISCIPLINE AND THE LAW OF ATTRACTION

The Law of Attraction is the ability to attract into our lives whatever we are focusing on. It might seem like an alien concept to some, but numerous scientific studies have verified it can work. The Law of Attraction is an ancient concept that we have the ability to influence and create our life events.

If you use the law of attraction or generally feel good with yourself. You might have noticed these kinds of things happen:

- You seem to have "good luck," and it keeps coming your way.
- You forge friendly partnerships at work and create closer bonds with your family.

- You are happy with all the positive things in your life, making you think more positive thoughts, and so on.

On the other hand, if you don't feel good and give off negative vibes, you might have experienced some of the following things.

- Future business partners and colleagues pick up on your negative vibes and avoid you.
- You seem unapproachable, as your body language repels people.
- When things go wrong, it feels like everything is going wrong. You feel like you are stuck in a rut.

If you think about it, it makes perfect sense. If you feel down and depressed, your mind is not sending out any positive vibes, and neither is your body. This can affect your motivation and your general zest for your life.

You can feel like the whole world is against you and feel stuck where you are.

Flipping this on its head and approaching things more positively and happily can instantly change things around. Not only does your head feel calmer, but so does your body. Even the word "disease" is saying that you are not at ease. So, give your body the release it needs and start using discipline to think more positively.

However, while the Law of Attraction can work, something far outweighs and can guarantee your success will become real. It is discipline.

Discipline will be there holding your hand and will keep you going.

There is nothing to stop you from using discipline with the Law of Attraction. Anything that makes you feel happy and positive is definitely worth doing. But on those days when something bad happens, again and again, and you find it difficult to harness the Law of Attraction, discipline will be there holding your hand and keeping you going.

THE BODY AND MIND CONNECTION

There is no denying that there is a strong connection between the body and mind. A systematic review at the University of Canberra Research Institute found regular physical exercise in over 50s can improve cognitive function. In fact, the results were so good that the scientists recommended that the over 50s should exercise as often as possible.

Research has also shown that walking 10,000 steps for 100 days in a row can increase your mental health and overall wellbeing. This research has prompted many campaigns to get people walking regularly to help their mental health. It is the reason why many neurologists and psychiatrists recommend walking to patients.

But the connection does not stop there. Think about the last time you lost your temper. I bet it makes you feel weird and slightly uncomfortable, thinking about it. Nobody likes to lose their temper. Sometimes we can create terrible situations from a small argument.

We can "explode" outwardly, and it can affect us mentally and physically.

However, by using discipline, we can tame our emotions inside our head and stop ourselves from hurting ourselves. We can learn to control our anger and react more calmly. This can keep our blood pressure in check and eliminate problems like headaches, and irritable bowel syndrome, which all come from stress.

It gives you control in your life. If you are prone to being impulsive in decisions and speaking, discipline can make you think before you act.

If you think back to the last chapter, you can see many mental techniques you can use to help your body. The body and mind connection is apparent, and if you want to reach your goals and be a success, you need to consider both of them. Discipline can help you in all areas of your life, and your body and mind thrive from it. You can learn to be free as a bird, with nothing weighing you down.

CHAPTER FOUR - ACTION STEP

In this chapter, we have discussed the importance of our mental health and what we can do to support it. We have learnt about different techniques and how we can easily apply them in our lives. We have also discussed the body and mind connection and how they are both important for our self-care.

This is the fourth action step. All of the action steps are equally important. Therefore, it is best to take your time and only move on when you are ready.

- Go back to the mindfulness section and try the Body Scan and Walking meditations.
- Think about 3 things in your life that make you feel stressed and give you negative thoughts. Write down goals related to these stress-related thoughts, so you can work towards eliminating them from your life.
- Spend 24 hours thinking only positive thoughts and notice the change in your behaviour to others and how you feel inside you.

You can now move on to the next chapter to find out how to create effective habits and reach your goals using your discipline.

5

COHABIT WITH HABITS

"Good habits are the key to all success."

— OG MANDINO

Now we understand what discipline is and how it relates to our mental and physical health. But how can we build our precious discipline to achieve what we want? Habit creation is the answer. It can help you create a happy and healthy life by creating the best habits and eliminating the bad ones.

Habits are key to gaining personal freedom and becoming a better version of yourself. They are instrumental in building that essential self-discipline. So we can keep going long-term until we reach our goals.

Think of the negative impact that bad habits have had on you.

Some bad habits might have been a factor throughout your whole life, but you didn't know how to shake them off. We hear about bad habits and how they affect our lives. But creating good habits are sometimes overlooked.

THE IMPORTANCE OF HABITS IN YOUR LIFE

Good habits can be far-reaching and make a real positive difference. It's not only the ritual of performing a daily habit. They can affect how we present ourselves to the world. Also, how we interact with others and react to different situations.

Imagine how influential good habits can be in your life.

Habits Can Define Your Character

Habits can form your character. As an example, if you start using healthy habits, your character will become more healthy. It will feel like your natural self. You will start making healthy choices without even thinking about it.

Help You To Reach Your Goals

You can use daily habits to help you achieve the goals you have set for yourself. It is not something that is going to happen overnight. So using a daily habit will help you inch ever closer to your goal every single day.

Habits Are Flexible

It doesn't matter if you have never used habits to your advantage before. You can start from scratch and redefine yourself. You can change all those annoying bad habits that make you feel depressed. Nothing is set in stone, and neither are habits.

Create A Solid Foundation

Whatever it is you want to change or achieve in your life, you have to start somewhere. Habits are an easy way to start, as whatever they are, you become it. Akin to building a house that needs to have a solid base, so does your personal development. Habits give you a solid foundation, so you can also use your inner self-discipline.

Use It As An Alternative To Motivation

If you remember, back in the second chapter. We learnt that there were two different motivation types. If either of them fails us, we can rely on our habits instead. On those days when we don't feel bothered to do anything, our habit makes us do it instead.

IT'S A WORLD FULL OF BRAIN LOVING HABITS

Habits are more common than you probably think. Even if you haven't consciously created a habit before, you are using them all the time. In fact, more than 40% of the actions you perform each day are habits and not decisions.

Research in 2020 at Dartmouth College found some interesting results concerning habit creation. When the brain starts to develop a new habit, there is a sudden burst of activity. This activity happens in as little as half a second in the dorsolateral striatum part of the brain. The researchers found that this brain activity increases as the habit becomes stronger.

Habits also create neurological cravings. When you carry out a certain type of behaviour, your brain rewards you with a release of "pleasure" chemicals. Consequently, the more you activate the habit, the stronger it becomes until it is automatic. With such a strong effect, you must pick good habits, as it can be hard to break the bad ones.

THE HABIT LOOP

The best way to understand how habits work is to look at the Habit Loop. It is a neurological loop and is demonstrated below.

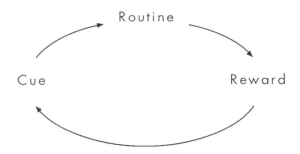

- The first part is the *Cue,* or sometimes it is referred to as the trigger. It can be many different things: a feeling, a location, certain people, or even a set time of the day.
- The second part of the loop is the *Routine*. This is the thing that you normally do. For example, biting your nails, eating chocolate, smoking, etc.
- The third part of the loop is the *Reward*. The reward is when you feel the chemicals released in your brain because of your routine.

The process continues in a loop because of the reward that you receive. It is referred to as a self-reinforcing mechanism, as eventually, it becomes automatic. The brain stops getting involved in decision-making because the habit has "taken over".

Habits become encoded in our brains' structure. It saves us time and energy, as we don't need to relearn anything.

When you understand how the Habit Loop works, you can change parts of the cycle to break negative habits and create positive ones instead.

HOW TO HARNESS THE POWER OF THE HABIT LOOP

The possibilities are endless when it comes to habit creation. Give yourself the best life by creating positive habits that match your aspirations. Unless you take charge and actively want to change a bad habit, every time a cue or trigger is activated, it will keep happening over and over again. If you want to change it, you need to change the routine.

As wonderful as it is, your brain cannot tell the difference between bad and good habits. You have to change the routines or actions to enable new positive habits. It is important to note that you never eliminate a bad habit; you replace it with a new one.

All you have to do is:

1. Use the same cue
2. *Change the routine.*
3. You receive the same reward.

It is not a difficult process, and as soon as you have changed one bad habit, you can keep going.

Psychological evidence around habit formation has been published in the British Journal of General Practice. It advises habit formation is simple for people to implement, and it has real potential for long-term impact.

For example, you might be a smoker and associate smoking a cigarette straight after having finished a meal. You can change the routine and do something else after the meal. Over time the habit will develop and stick. Soon, you will be following the new habit automatically.

Or maybe in the morning, the first thing you do is check your emails. The chemical release in the brain is the satisfaction that you have checked them. However, you could change the routine to something more calming. Instead of checking your emails do 30 minutes of exercise instead. You will still receive your reward and feel fit in the process.

CREATE GOOD HABITS IN ALL AREAS OF YOUR LIFE

Balance is essential in life. You can create habits that look after your health, but don't limit yourself. You can use them for everything. This includes your relationships, your work, and even your spirituality. There is no limit to habit creation, and that is what makes them so useful.

When you start setting up your new routines and create better habits, you become more productive.

You start to realise which actions are the most important for you. Habits help you become a better version of yourself, especially when you attach specific goals to your habits and routines. Your focus means you always know what is a priority in your life. You get things done and are always moving towards your goal.

ENJOY YOUR MINI ACHIEVEMENTS

Habits take time to stick in your brain. Some people claim that it takes 21 days, or even as short as 7 days, for habits to change and take permanent effect. This is not the case, as there is no set time period. A 2009 study published in the European Journal of Social Psychology found it can take anything from 18 days to 254 days to form a habit completely.

This is because everybody is an individual and processes things at their own pace. Consequently, it is so important to celebrate your mini achievements as you work with new habits. Give yourself a proverbial pat on the back every time you change your routine. Feel the difference and enjoy it.

A GUIDE TO DEVELOPING THE SELF-DISCIPLINE HABIT

Now is the time to start developing your self-discipline habits. If you already use some form of self-discipline, this is great. But there is always more you can learn and do. Personal development is not short term. It's a process that lasts your whole lifetime.

Why Starting Small Works Best

You don't need to rush when it comes to discipline. It is a long-term strategy. It is best to take your time and do it right. Start small and build it from there. Your habits don't have to be huge. It is more important to be consistent than to pick a large habit and put yourself under pressure. So, be proactive and pick habits that are not too big, so you don't become stressed and start viewing them as a burden.

Here are some examples of smaller habits compared to big ones:

- Walking for 15 minutes every day, instead of 1 hour of exercise every day.
- Visit one family member a week instead of trying to see everybody in a week.
- Saving 5% of your salary, instead of 50%.

By having a large goal and small habits to reach it, you can achieve success. Your daily habits will automatically keep you on track to help you get there and reach your goal.

Use Behaviour Chains To Make It Feel More Real

You can also use behaviour chains to help you write down clear instructions for your routine. So, for example, instead of a vague, "I need to do some exercises every day." You can instead use "When I come home after my working day, I will change into my workout clothes, chill for half an hour, then go for a walk".

When everything is clear about what needs to be done, you can complete it successfully. You won't be distracted by doing something else and then breaking your habit. Behaviour chains can give you clear guidance to make sure you follow through on your new habit.

Eliminate Your Triggers

In the Habit Loop, cues (triggers) can negatively affect you. All your effort can be for nothing, and before you know it, you have broken your habit. So you don't end up in this situation, it is worth sitting down and having a serious think about your triggers. Ask yourself what it is that causes you to want to break your habit.

Once you know what it is, you can eliminate the trigger.

Consider using anything that can help you stick to your habit. For example, your goal might be to reduce your screen time overall. One of your habits for this could be to spend less time on your mobile. You can help yourself by placing the mobile in a different room in the evening, so the temptation is out of sight.

Control Your Urges

It is normal to get urges to stop what you are doing. When this happens, you can use your inner self-discipline and elements of mindfulness to resist those urges. Set yourself a certain length of time to do some work. For example, 10 minutes to write up a report, do a walk, do some meditation, or whatever task you want to do.

In those 10 minutes, you can only do that specific task, nothing else.

So, if you feel the urge to do some internet surfing or check your mobile, you can't. You will have to sit there and do nothing. It shows your internal urges, who is the real boss. You aren't going to be swayed by distractions and temptations. You will stay focused on the routine/activity at hand.

It is an easy way for you to monitor your urges when trying to complete a specific task. This "reality check" is a fascinating insight. As you become more mindful of your urges, it makes you more focused on your task.

Give Your Urges A Workout

You can further develop this system by subjecting your urges to interval training. It is like a form of training, which, over time, helps to develop your self-discipline. Follow these steps:

1. Set yourself the task that you want to do. For example, exercising, studying, writing, etc.
2. Set your timer for 10 minutes. (Eventually, you can increase this time period).
3. Start on the task. If you get any urges, you need to stop and do nothing. Or, if you are feeling strong, carry on with the task.
4. When your timer goes off after ten minutes, you can have a rest for 5 minutes.
5. Then after your break, get back to the task and repeat the process.
6. You can do this interval training for an hour and see how you get on, and then increase this period over time.

The beauty of interval training is that you can achieve a lot and look at your urges. This insider information is invaluable to look at further habit creation or to remove triggers.

Break Out Of Your Comfort Zone And Feel The Difference

It is easy for us to deliberately avoid uncomfortable things and carry on in our little bubble. This isn't good for our self-discipline as we are not putting ourselves into challenging situations. Sometimes the easy option seems less troublesome, so we carry on doing the same thing.

Break out from your comfort bubble and try new things.

If we want to grow and achieve our dreams, we need to do things we have never done before. It allows us to stretch our mind and realise how much more we are capable of doing. Of course, there will be failures on the way, but that is how we keep learning.

Failures help us to keep growing. The experience alone is worth trying something new. Even if it feels a little uncomfortable at first, it won't seem as daunting the second time, and so on. You'll realise that it isn't as bad as you thought it was going to be. In fact, in most cases, the positives far outweigh the negatives.

True grit and determination to try new things are a sure way to fire up your magical self-discipline.

- You will have done/learnt something new.
- It will have opened your mind to other possibilities and opportunities.
- You realise how strong you can be, which pushes you further.

CREATE A MORNING ROUTINE

Another way to guarantee your success is to create routines that can help you use your discipline. Win the morning, and you win the day. We have more control of our time in the morning so use it wisely. Get up earlier than normal and schedule in a routine. Make it a priority to do your most important task first thing. Whether that be going for a run, to the gym, writing your book, or finishing off your project.

Getting up early has also been proven scientifically to work in your favour. Research shared in the Journal of Applied Social Psychology found that <u>morning people are more proactive and happier.</u>

Many highly successful people make that extra bit of effort to get up earlier than the rest of us. Their <u>morning habits help them with their successes.</u> Plus, over time, they don't need to use any effort to see the benefits all around them. So, what can you put into your morning routine to make it worthwhile for you?

1. Try waking up naturally, without an alarm clock. Jeff Bezos, Amazon CEO, swears by this, and so does Oprah.
2. Start exercising as soon as you get up. Bill Gates multitasks and watches DVDs while he is on the treadmill. It doesn't have to be for hours. Only 10-15 minutes can give your body that positive exercise buzz and get the blood flowing.

3. Self-reflection is a great way to get yourself pumped up for the day ahead. Steve Jobs used to look in a mirror and ask himself, "If today were the last day of my life, would I want to do what I am about to do today?". He said that if the answer ended up being no for several days in a row, then he would make a change.
4. Instead of reaching for a caffeine fix, have a glass of water instead. Cameron Diaz has a litre of water as soon as she gets up to set her up for the day.
5. Don't start looking at your emails, or checking your mobile, or anything related to tech. If you don't exercise, then opt for some relaxing meditation to connect with your body.
6. Spend 15 minutes reading something that stimulates you. It will help to get your brain swinging into action, and you might receive some life-changing ideas.

CREATE A NIGHT ROUTINE

A night routine is just as important as a morning routine. Let your body and mind enjoy a wind-down before you go to bed. It has been on the go all day, AND it needs to have some signals to help it relax.

1. Create a to-do list the night before. It will save you time in the morning, and you are already mentally preparing yourself for the next day. It also puts a line underneath your work for that day. It is like a signal to the brain that the workday has finished.
2. Similar to the morning routine, avoid caffeine. You certainly don't need a buzz when you are about to go to bed. Stop drinking it at least 6-8 hours before you go to bed.
3. Avoid blue light, and don't look at your mobile, PC, television for a few hours beforehand.
4. Write a positive, personal message for yourself to inspire you for the morning.
5. Make sure you get at least 6-8 hours of sleep.
6. Drink a nice relaxing tea, such as camomile, to calm your body and mind.

CHECK YOUR HABITS AND REFINE THEM

Any habit or routine will work best when using a reflective loop. You need to assess if the habit is working continually. If it isn't, you need to take action to refine it. By checking your habits regularly, you have a higher chance of success.

It is up to you how often you check them. This could be weekly, monthly, or bimonthly. It will help you determine how well you are doing, working towards your goal. But IT would be best if you were asking yourself the following questions:

1. Why am I making this habit? How is it going to help me?
2. Is this habit working? Do I need to refine it, so it helps me achieve my goal?
3. Should I stop this habit?

The last question might seem a bit strange, but it is important. Sometimes it is necessary to stop some habits if you realise they are not helping you achieve your goal. It might have been a bad habit to pick, or it doesn't help your goal any more.

REMEMBER THE REASON WHY

There may be times when you still struggle. When you experience these moments, don't feel down about it, it is normal to have moments of doubt. If this happens, think back to why you are making the habit.

- What is your big goal?
- Why did you decide to create the habit?

Reminding yourself of the answers to these two questions can help you get your focus back. It will give you the reality check that you need at that moment.

CHAPTER FIVE - ACTION STEP

We now know how important habits are in our lives and how we can use them to build our self-discipline. We have also learnt how to create habits and manage them in our daily routine. Additionally, how morning and night routines can help us to fine-tune our discipline.

In this action step, you will create your first habits to help you reach your goal/goals in life.

- Go back to Chapter One and look at the goal/goals that you listed. Think about the goal/goals and break them down into "bite-size" amounts. Use the habit loop to create a positive habit related to one of your goals.
- Get out of your comfort zone for a day. Try doing a task that you don't like doing but you know will be beneficial for you. Analyse how you felt before doing it and how you felt afterwards.
- Use interval training on an important task for 1 hour. Try doing the task for 10 minutes at a

time. With 5 minute breaks. NB When your 10-minute sessions start, either do the task or nothing at all.

A MILLION DOLLARS TODAY OR A PENNY A DAY DOUBLED FOR 30 DAYS?

"A daily routine built on good habits and disciplines separates the most successful among us from everyone else."

— DARREN HARDY

When you create a daily routine, everything starts to fit into place. Your dedication to achieving your goal starts to materialise in front of you. You can feel and see the effects of following your routine and keeping your good habits. This approach and the transformation that happens is gradual but life-changing.

Little steps forward will always serve you better.

Some days you might not feel like doing anything. We all get days like that, but that's where your discipline and daily routine will support you. It takes time. There is no overnight transformation. It all takes a disciplined and consistent approach to your objective, but you will get there.

USING A PENNY TO BECOME A MILLIONAIRE

When you feel ready to improve yourself and your life, you might feel an urge to get going quickly. Quick fixes do work but are normally only short-term solutions. If you want to make lasting change in your life, it is better to work on long-term solutions.

It is the point where your new routine, positive habits and magical discipline all meet together.

You have a structure in place that is supporting you to reach your goals. If you stick with it, you will get there. A great way to demonstrate a long-term investment in yourself is the penny doubled over 30 days concept. The scenario is:

You can receive $1 million upfront or opt for a penny instead to double it every day for 30 days. The penny option will make $5 million after the 30 days. Which option would you pick? Would you like money upfront, or are you in it for the long game?

You might think $5 million seems far-fetched, but here is the calculation so that you can see it in practice:

Day 1: $0.01	**Day 2:** $0.02	**Day 3:** $0.04
Day 4: $0.08	**Day 5:** $0.16	**Day 6:** $0.32
Day 7: $0.64	**Day 8:** $1.28	**Day 9:** $2.56
Day 10: $5.12	**Day 11:** $10.24	**Day 12:** $20.48
Day 13: $40.96	**Day 14:** $81.92	**Day 15:** $163.84
Day 16: $327.68	**Day 17:** $655.36	**Day 18:** $1,310.72
Day 19: $2,621.44	**Day 20:** $5,242.88	**Day 21:** $10,485.76
Day 22: $20,971.52	**Day 23:** $41,943.04	**Day 24:** $83,886.08
Day 25: $167,772.16	**Day 26:** $335,544.32	**Day 27:** $671,088.64
Day 28: $1,342,177.28	**Day 29:** $2,684,354.56	**Day 30:** $5,368,709.12

In this particular case, it is related to money. Other factors can affect your money. Such as the influence of taxes and the fluctuation of shares. But you can get a sense of the general idea. You can use this concept for any goals you are working towards in your life.

Prepare yourself to work for long-term gain instead of a short-term option. Continuous effort and persistence might seem hard in the beginning. You might feel like you are not getting anywhere fast. However, you are making leaps and bounds without even realising it. There will also come the point further down the line when you can gather incredible momentum.

It all relates to the power of compound interest.

Another point worth bearing in mind is that it isn't only about doubling your money. For example, if you stopped the financial example on day 26, you would only receive $335,544.32.

You can also expect the same results for any long-term goal or project. The rewards are far greater if you stick with the system. As discussed earlier in the book, keep your focus on your original goal instead of settling for a second-best option.

Small Steps Lead To Big Changes

When you are in the thick of it, you might be thinking that nothing is happening. However, in reality, there is always a lot going on behind the scenes. It's similar to the old proverb my beautiful mom used to say to me, *"Look after the pennies, and the pounds will look after themselves"*.

As you can see from the monetary example, they certainly do. It's also the same in your life. When you take small steps, use your new good habits, morning and night routines, and discipline. They all combine to give you the perfect support system to change your life for the better.

WHAT IS THE COMPOUND EFFECT?

Darren Hardy was the author of The Compound Effect, a New York Times and Wall Street Journal bestseller. He based the book on his own experiences and interviews with some of the world's most successful people. *The Compound Effect* can help you to shape your destiny based on your life decisions. These little decisions can create the life you desire if you make the right ones.

The compound effect, in essence, is a long-term strategy you can use to gain huge rewards from making small, consistent actions.

If you use the system, it is possible to multiply your successes and keep advancing. To do this, you need to chart your progress and make any necessary changes along the way. It also takes time and patience to achieve it.

Creating The Right Ripples In Your Life

In his book, Hardy states that consistency is the key to success. All the successful people he interviewed shared one thing. They all consistently made smart choices over long periods. It all relates to the Law of Cause and Effect. This Law is one of the 12 Universal Laws that can help you to manifest your dreams.

The Law of Cause and Effect states there is a similar resulting consequence for every action you make.

- For example, if you opt to meditate for 10 minutes in the morning. You will naturally feel calmer as part of your morning routine. In comparison, if you decided to spend the same time on social media. You are only browsing and not doing anything productive, and it could lead to you feeling lazy.
- Also, think about the times when you have lost your temper. You felt terrible afterwards, and your body feels hurt, not forgetting the negative thoughts in your head. But think back to a time when you have helped somebody out, not expecting anything in return. It made you feel great inside that you could help somebody.

When you start using this with your goals and make the right decisions, your small steps create positive feelings and situations.

Then, when you add the compounding effect into the equation, you can see the amazing benefits that will come your way. As Hardy mentions in his book, it takes time and patience to achieve your goals. But you can use the Law of Cause and Effect to your advantage in life. Taking all this into account, you can see how powerful daily choices can be.

When we make our decisions and choices, we don't realise what a lasting effect these can have on our lives. Hardy encourages us to make "conscious choices", so the Compound Effect can work positively in our favour.

You reap what you sow in life, but you can reap more than you are sowing if you use the compound effect to your advantage.

So we have incredible power to change our life by making the right choices and decisions. When we do this, step-by-step, our choices shape what our actions will be. These actions become habits, and with practice, we can make them permanent in our lives.

It's Time To Take Responsibility

We can sail through life and not worry about the consequences of our actions. But if you want to develop and create the best version of yourself. You need to change this approach and start making conscious decisions. If you do this, you can stay on track with your goals.

Every positive decision or choice you make will take you one step closer to your life goals.

Also, it's not only about your goals. You can take responsibility for all the things in your life. Conscious decision making can help you take responsibility for:

- Your relationships with your different family members, friends, and colleagues and how you interact with them.

- The mistakes that you have made in your life and the lessons you have learnt from them. So you can learn from them, instead of making the same mistakes.
- The luck in your life is in your control. You can't use it as an excuse, as it is a sum of your action, attitude, preparation, and opportunities.
- Choose the life that you want first, and then consider your business/career in second place. This order will ensure that you create the best lifestyle for yourself.

Using The Magic Of Momentum

"The accomplishment of any goal is the progressive accumulation, or compound effect, of small steps taken consistently over time."

— DARREN HARDY

Have you ever worked on a hard project that seemed like everything was leading to disaster? But it ended up working after lots of stress and bluster. I bet this rings a bell. Well, imagine, in comparison, working towards your goal/goals in small steps, without stress and at a more relaxed pace. It sounds a lot nicer. This system is exactly how the compound effect will help you.

You can build your momentum by mastering your daily routines. Regardless of how you feel in the morning or the night, you need to follow your routines without fail. This consistency gives you total control of your mornings and your evenings. You know what to do and when to do it.

Remember to change parts of your routine if they are not producing the right results.

It is good to be consistent, but it is more important to be positively consistent. If you notice something in your routine that doesn't seem to give you powerful results, you can change it. Don't be scared to do this. Swap it to something positive for you.

The journey is more exciting than the destination.

By now, you have a system in place for your morning and evening routines. You can step this up a bit by looking at your weekly, monthly, and quarterly results. You can track your activity and habits at these different points to see if you are on track. If not, you can adjust them accordingly.

This monitoring system helps you keep an eye on your habits, so you are always moving forward. Remember to keep the habits small and don't overdo them by creating too many. These little steps all keep your momentum moving on.

Jump Over Obstacles Like An Olympic Hurdler

The system works, but there will be times when challenges and obstacles arise. These are normal in life, and it doesn't mean you are doing anything wrong. This point is when you need to dig in deep and keep going. It is the time when most people give up on their dreams and goals.

Hardy encourages us to view any challenges or obstacles as opportunities for us. When we commit ourselves and use our discipline to overcome these hurdles, we can grow even further as a result.

The chances are, obstacles will push us out of our comfort zone at times.

When these situations occur, we need to take the plunge and step into the unknown. These moments are when we grow the most. We start learning new things and realise that we can handle them, and it is not as scary as we originally thought. Also, when we start learning new abilities and skills, it opens us up for greater opportunities.

All the consistent good choices we have made so far prepare us for the obstacles. The challenges won't seem as daunting as we know the differences between good and bad choices. So we are more prepared to handle these problems when they arise. In fact, over time, you might view them with excitement instead of dread.

Think about how many people give up when the hurdles seem too big.

That is the reason why there are only a few highly successful people. These people are prepared to jump all the hurdles and run to the finish line. If you can change your mindset and decide you want to jump every single hurdle, you will gain even more in your life.

USING THE COMPOUND EFFECT WITH YOUR GOALS AND HABITS

It can be easy to get caught up in too much habit and goal creation and get a bit lost. The easiest way to do it is to break it down into stages.

Stage 1

Sit down and set specific goals. Double-check your goals. Do they still make sense to you? Are they specific enough? If not, change them so that everything is clear for the compound effect to work well.

Stage 2

Write down all the tasks that you need to do to reach each of your goals. Then change these tasks into good habits that you can follow every day.

Stage 3

Check what you are doing each day and plan your habits/tasks to match what you need to do.

Stage 4

At the end of each day, look at your habits and see if you managed to follow them.

Don't spend too long on this task as you are already monitoring your results every week, month or bimonthly. But it is still a good quick check to see how you are doing.

PRACTISING GRATITUDE

Gratitude can also play an important part in our lives and increase the compound effect even further. At times, we take things in our life for granted. The people we love, our careers, our friends, our general lives.

But remembering to be grateful for these special things in our life can sprinkle more magic on the Law of Cause and Effect.

Incorporate it into your morning or evening routine, say a thank you in your head, speak out loud, or write it on paper.

Express your gratitude for the things you have in your life. This thanks can also extend to your daily tasks. Be gracious with your daily communications and interactions, and thank people for their assistance, attention, time.

From the lady or gentleman in the supermarket. Or the little bird who hops in front of you on your walk. Thank them all, and they will be grateful. This positive energy and attention will come straight back to you when you least expect it.

THE CHINESE BAMBOO TREE

One of the most dynamic motivational speakers, Les Brown, gave a short speech about the Chinese Bamboo Tree. It was a speech that sums up the compound effect in a beautiful way. The *Chinese Bamboo Tree* story is a parable related to how we can grow as a person. Working toward your goals can take time, and it might not seem like anything is happening, but it is.

It is all about cultivating patience and knowing that you will reach your goals.

So how are we similar to the Chinese bamboo tree? Well, here are some of the main takeaways from the story:

- The Chinese bamboo tree needs certain elements to nurture it so that it can grow. It needs fertile soil, sun, and water. This need to be nurtured is the same for us. If we want to be successful, we need to look after ourselves mentally and physically. We have to do actions and create habits that help us to move forward. In the 1st year, you might not see any signs of development.
- In the second, third and fourth years, the Chinese bamboo tree still doesn't show any growth above the soil. The local people in the story think that the farmer is not thinking straight. You might have experienced this from people telling you that your development is all in vain. It is understandable. They might think this when they cannot see anything happening, after all the hard work you have put in.
- The farmer starts questioning his own belief in growing his plant and wonders if his neighbours are right. Maybe his idea is silly? The same happens to us in our development. We start questioning our dreams, ideas, hopes, and even the system. This time is normally the point when people give up, but it is also the turning point.

- The farmer persists, and in the 5th year, the Chinese bamboo tree erupts from the ground. It grows 30m in only six weeks!

But the real question here is, did the tree grow so quickly in six weeks? The answer is no. Because there was so much going on behind the scenes, or in this case, under the ground.

The tree created a root system, a stable foundation to grow and support itself in the 5th year. This foundational support is the same for us. If we can create a solid foundation over a long period, we have a higher chance of success. Additionally, it can also help us sustain our success.

When we work hard towards our dreams and goals, we have to encounter challenges that make us stronger.

Our foundation is stronger as a result. So, when we receive the success we have worked so hard to attain, there is less chance of us losing it. Additionally, if the farmer dug into the ground to see if the seed was growing, he would have affected the tree's growth. The tree would not be as strong.

The same situation applies to us if we let criticisms and negativity affect us. Or keep changing our systems completely instead of sticking to them. We end up creating confusion and stunting our personal development.

Like Les Brown says, there are no instant results in personal development. You have to keep watering your dream until you get there. During all this time, our progress might seem frustrating, slow, and at times unrewarding. But through this experience, we are building our character and 0ur courage to grow even further.

CHAPTER SIX - ACTION STEP

In this chapter, we have learnt about *The Compound Effect*. You will now have a better understanding of how consistent action, over the long-term, provides the best results. So you can start putting this effect into practice, work your way through the next action step, which is detailed below.

Now you will create your sixth action steps.

- Write down three positive steps that you can implement in your life that will improve your relationships. Vow to consistently follow them.
- Identify areas in your life that used to be successful but that no longer work. Create new goals and habits to help you in these specific areas.
- Practice gratitude by writing down something you are grateful for at the end of each day.

VALENTINE'S DAY - ALL DAY, EVERY DAY

"Enjoy the journey of life and not just the endgame."

— BENEDICT CUMBERBATCH

You know that lovely warm glow you feel inside of you on Valentine's day. Well, imagine feeling that every day of your life. It's easy for us to only concentrate on our goal. But the process itself is as rewarding. When you start enjoying the process, every day is Valentine's day.

You might have already made several attempts to reach your goals, for it to all end in failure. It is soul-destroying when you fail, and the pain is sometimes hard to put into words. You then find the strength to rebuild your confidence and self-esteem "to have another go". But then you hit some huge obstacles along the way, give up and fail all over again. Sound familiar?

Nobody likes this negative stop-start cycle that breaks our self-esteem.

We all want to be successful, but sometimes our ideas, plans, routines and discipline all go out of the window. What goes wrong? How do you keep ending up in this position? It's the pressure we put on ourselves to reach our goals. Instead of relaxing and enjoying the life-changing journey

THE IMAGINARY PRESSURE INSIDE OUR HEADS

So, what kinds of pressure do we face? Also, are they real or imagined? Most, if not all, of the pressure, is imaginary. If we follow our routines by using our habits and check our process, there is nothing left to do. But these kinds of imaginary pressures can arise:

1. Everything is taking too long because I am too slow or not clever enough.
2. I keep bumping into obstacles. I might as well give up.

3. I broke my routine, so I might as well stop now.
4. It is harder than I thought. I am not up to this.
5. I am going to fail yet again.
6. What's the point? I can't see any immediate results.

I am sure that you have had some of these negative thoughts, or maybe all of them. It is more common than you probably think. So, how can you get around these thoughts and succeed?

You need to fall in love with the process.

You have a process. You have taken the time to create it. You know your specific goals, have set up routines and use your habits and discipline to get there. It's not a rigid, ugly system designed to switch you off. You have created it to make the journey to success to be as comfortable as possible. Sure, you will always have challenges on the way, but these are all necessary to create the best version of yourself.

LOVE THE PROCESS MORE THAN THE RESULTS

Of course, you can't wait to reach your results, but by now, you realise that it is a long-term process. You have to be patient. By loving the process more than the results, it can help you get into the groove. It will also help to level out your patience levels, so you enjoy your life right now. Instead of being super serious until you hit your target, cherish the journey.

Why not enjoy these changes at the time and embrace the person you have become.

You might remember the famous quote, "Life is what happens to us while we are making other plans." Many people attribute the quote to John Lennon, but he was only 17 when the quote first appeared in Reader's Digest in 1957 and was made by Allen Saunders.

The quote demonstrates how important it is to enjoy your life, especially if you are making firm plans for the future. We can get caught up in goals and desired results. We forget about enjoying the process of getting there. As you grow and change as a person, you learn so much about yourself and the world around you. You do need to use discipline if you want to achieve your goal/goals.

But always remember to keep fun in the equation.

- It doesn't matter if you are on Day One of your workout at the gym. You might have a long way to go to get to your ideal weight or to tone yourself up. But don't stress out about the

result. Enjoy the time in the gym as you workout and the nice feeling in your body after. Also, your mind will feel more alert.
- The course you are currently doing to further your career. You could be 50% of the way through it, and you are itching to finish it. But don't rush. Do it at your designated time and enjoy it. Be present and learn the information properly.
- Or perhaps you have started doing an early morning routine and hate going outside in the cold. Ignore these thoughts and look around you. Check out the wildlife, the rising sun, and the world waking up. You would be missing all this is if you stayed in bed or walked with your negative feelings about the cold.

Whatever you are doing in your process. It is all part and parcel of the bigger picture. The little, individual segments are all as rewarding if you can take them for what they are. They are little stepping stones as you progress in life. These stones are also interesting, not only your destination.

Extra Benefits Are Waiting For You

When you start to love the process, extra benefits can appear in your life. It sometimes feels like magic, but your belief in the process is waving the magic wand. Here are some of the things you might experience:

1. You start to realise what works and what doesn't. For example, if you plough on towards your goals and succeed, you might not know how you got there. You might have been able to do it differently with less stress.
2. You can appreciate the results more if you understand the process. You will have failures and obstacles along the way. Learning how to turn failures into opportunities are valuable learning experiences. When you get to your goal, you will be more "streetwise" and will appreciate how much hard work you did to get there.
3. Of course, you will feel incredible when you hit your goal/goals. But you can have mini feelings of euphoria as you are working through your process. You will learn new things about yourself and how to do things differently. These are all useful "tools of the trade" that you pick up along the way and can enjoy at the time.
4. You will enjoy being in the moment more. A good example is hand washing dirty dishes. It is a process. You have a pile of dirty dishes that need to be cleaned. When you clean them, be in

the moment. Feel the soapy mixture on your hands. Smell it. Listen to the sound of splashing water. Enjoy the look of the dishes when they are clean. It's a whole new experience of enjoying different processes.

DON'T BE AN ACHIEVEMENT ADDICT

For most of us, this won't be our first rodeo on working towards personal development goals. Chances are you have already achieved some goals in your life. This book will help you to enhance your process. It will also make your goal-achieving less stressful and more fun. But some people are "achievement addicts."

These people are usually pushed for time, set constant goals and go full out to achieve them asap.

They tick the latest goal they have achieved off their list and quickly move on to the next one. But if you were to ask them what they have learned along the way, they might feel a little confused. These achievement addicts are only in it for the goal fix at the end.

It's a bit like completing a bucket list on overdrive.

These people tend to find they are completely shattered after reaching their goal. It is no wonder they feel like that, with all the drive and energy it takes them to get to the end. But think about everything they are missing. In fact, are they developing at all?

Practice Self-Awareness

The slow, steady approach is best. Smell the roses along the way and savour every moment. If you do it this way, you will enjoy the result so much more. You will learn about your strengths, weaknesses, opportunities, and threats in more detail.

It allows you to tweak yourself along the way and become that better version of yourself.

You can spend time going into yourself and find out what is happening in there. Are you happy? Are you enjoying yourself? If you aren't, you know that you can address it and correct it. It's so much better than arriving at your goal and thinking, *"What was all that about?"*

Don't Avoid The Bad Things

Sometimes it isn't all hearts and rainbows in your life. You might have to do unpleasant things in your life to improve yourself. Plus, when you take the time to listen to your body and mind. You can find out what switches you on and off.

It might feel horrible confronting some bad things about yourself. But it is a lot better than rushing to the end goals and not addressing them. You will be no further forward than when you started.

These negative situations during the process can sometimes be the most rewarding to solve.

Use your inner discipline, grab the bull by the horns and find out what is going on there. Why do you feel the way you do? Is this "bad thing" part of you that you can change? Or is it something that you don't need to do, but you think you have to? You will be surprised what answers you get to these questions. It's important to remember to ask good questions of yourself and in turn you will get good answers.

TAKING THE TIME TO DO IT PROPERLY

You might think writing down specific goals and detailing the habits, routine and strategy you will use to get there can take up valuable time. But the actual process of writing everything down can improve your results.

A 2020 paper in Contemporary Educational Psychology found when students wrote about personal life goals and specified a strategy to attain them, their academic performance improved. The study done in two independent Universities found <u>writing down both academic and non-academic goals boosted academic performance by 22%.</u>

It is always best to write things down, and it doesn't matter what age you are. The research earlier on referred to students, but numerous studies with different ages back this up. A study conducted by a psychologist, Professor Gail Matthews, at the Dominican University of California found <u>people who wrote goals down were 20% more successful.</u>

Find Your Preferred Lifestyle Before Picking Your Goals

Ideally, it is best to pick your lifestyle before you pick your goals. Otherwise, you might reach your goal/goals and then decide you want something different. Think about the lifestyle you desire in life, and then create goals that match that lifestyle.

A Gallup poll in 2017 found that <u>only 15% of employees worldwide are engaged and enjoying their jobs</u>. It is an unfortunate statistic, as it seems so many people are doing jobs they don't enjoy or want. Instead of thinking about the lifestyle first and then the job afterwards.

For example, if you want to dedicate more time to your family, you might want to move more towards a part-time career. But if your goals are all career-related for high-flying jobs, is a part-time role realistic?

MAKE IT MAGICAL AND FUN

Deal with the boring tasks by making them more fun. If you have some tasks to do that make you feel bored, add a reward to them to make them more fun. Or ask a family member, friend, or colleague to compete with you. This healthy competition will keep you focused and make the task pass quickly. It might even help to change your mind about this particular task.

When you come up against a hard challenge, learn to laugh about it.

If you are too serious about accomplishing your goals, you might be attracting more obstacles. Laugh in the face of adversity, especially when working with others. You will feel less stressed, and it will help others around you as well. This is backed by science, as <u>social laughter can trigger the equivalent of an opioid release in humans.</u> You will also find fewer obstacles will come your way, thanks to the Law of Cause and Effect.

Step Crunch With Like-Minded People

Teamwork can help you. When you are working towards your goals, it doesn't have to be a solo quest. Sure, reaching your personal target is on you. But you can still hook up with people who might need to do the same steps. Think about some groups that match your development step and share that part of the journey with like-minded people.

- You will make new friends who are on your wavelength.
- You can see things from a different perspective.
- You will feel like you are not alone.
- It makes that individual step on your journey more exciting.

INCREASING YOUR SELF DISCIPLINE AND SELF ESTEEM

Sticking to your daily disciplines will make you proud of the person you will become and increase your self-esteem and confidence. As the one major way to increase your self-esteem and confidence is by keeping promises to yourself.

Vow not to break your promise to yourself.

If you always make sure you do the things you said you were going to do. Day by day, week by week, month by month and year on year, your daily disciplines will have a compound effect, and you will see the fruition of the seeds you sowed.

As an example, when I was younger, I trained as an amateur boxer. I ended up falling in love with the sweaty, intense training process. It was also quite amusing going into my regular bank job during the day with a bruised eye or swollen lip. Sometimes training felt like hard work, and in the early days, I questioned what on earth I was doing.

But it was all worthwhile because I stuck to the process.

After one year of training six times a week, Monday to Friday, and even on a Sunday, I was very athletic, lean, and happy. I was also able to increase my self-confidence, and my discipline was firing on all cylinders.

The whole process opened my mind to other possibilities and exciting opportunities. The more you can practice discipline and self-mastery, you will value yourself even more; by following your process.

Process-oriented people are more confident. Roger Staubach, a quarterback from the NFL, said, "*Confidence comes from hours and days and weeks and years of constant work and dedication."* This constant work and dedication are you following your process, being present and focusing on the details.

You will start to notice these changes in yourself:

- Your self-respect and pride will increase.
- You'll notice the change in the way that you hold your body and how you walk. You will stand tall with a straight back, projecting more confidence.
- You will feel more comfortable talking to new people as you are interested in learning more.
- You will get excited about new processes, as they seem like a new, exciting challenge instead of "a daily grind".

Trusting The Process

In Chapter Four, we learnt about mindfulness and meditation to keep our brain in the game. This is the chapter you can refer to if you do start to feel impatient. You can use some of the techniques there to recenter yourself and to enjoy the moment again. The process, when done properly, does take time to reach your goals. You might need to relax into the process again if you find that your mind is drifting. Don't give up. Be persistent and use your discipline to get back on track.

If we want the compound effect to work effectively, we have to trust the process.

Our self-discipline can hold us accountable so that we can keep going till we get there. It's those moments of doubt that can push us back and affect our self-confidence. When you throw yourself into the process, you are not swimming in high seas and hoping to survive. You are using a system that you know will work for you.

Enjoy the process and lay back in the sea on your unicorn lilo.

DON'T FORGET TO VISUALISE

Michael Phelps, the Olympic swimmer, has accredited using visualisation techniques to help him win races. He also uses it to prepare himself for any eventuality. So when those worse case scenarios, like water in his goggles, a ripped swimsuit or a bad start, happens, he can deal with it. Also, because he has trained his mind to think over the race so often, his body works on autopilot during races.

You don't have to be an Olympic athlete to manage this. Think and visualise throughout the process. Not only on the results but your daily habits and routines.

When you visualise, it can help you enjoy the process even more. You are getting a "taster session" of what will come to you later down the line. A true taste of success. It can help to keep you inspired. You can also keep enjoying that fuzzy Valentine's Day feeling.

It also doesn't hurt to think about how you will feel and look when you are a better version of yourself. The freedom from your current situation and living in a new world that you have created for yourself.

CHAPTER SEVEN - ACTION STEP

You have now finished reading Chapter Seven, and it is time to put into practice what you learned. You know that the process does not have to be hard work. You can view it as a useful support system that is always going to be there for you. Once you understand this, you can relax and enjoy the process even more.

Here are the action steps for the seventh chapter.

- Think about your current process and write down 3 things that you have enjoyed so far. It doesn't matter if some of them are small things.
- Look at your habits and goals. Check to see if there are any areas where you can "buddy-up" with somebody or join a group to help you complete a task.
- Be honest with yourself and think about your process. Is there anything in the process that you don't like? If so, set yourself the task to do it in the next week, without fail.

When you feel ready, you can move on to the next chapter.

8

MOVE THE NEEDLE

"The fact is, discipline is only punishment when imposed on you by someone else. When you discipline yourself, it's not punishment but empowerment."

— LES BROWN

If you want to create the best version of yourself and lead a fulfilling life, discipline will keep the fire burning inside of you. It is easy to give up one day and then find several days later from doing nothing; you have completely given up. Procrastination, laziness, excuses, and distractions.

They are all familiar words that can conspire against you.

A little movement in the right direction is better than standing still, or worse, going backwards.

It's important to keep going, regardless of how you feel, your mood, or the planets' alignment. You are in charge of your destiny; nobody else. Your success is in your hands alone. It can be a lonely path at times, but it is a path you need to keep following to push yourself to greater things.

Les Brown hits the nail on the head with his quote above. Self-discipline is not punishment. It is pure empowerment.

You might have days when you feel like throwing your hands in the air and giving up. You know those days when everything you do or touch goes wrong. Don't let these days "break you". These are special days that can give you valuable lessons. When they happen, analyse what went wrong.

- Is there a pattern?
- Could you have done something differently?
- Did you react in the wrong way?
- Are you doing too much?
- Did you misunderstand something?

Ask yourself these questions and see if they can give you any clues. The answers will help you understand what you need to learn. Chances are, these days are your turning points. On the days when you are so close to giving up, you can find out so much about yourself.

These days are your best days in disguise.

View them as a bend in your path, which will lead you on to something better. It might not seem like it at the time, but keep going. Sometimes we might end up on a different journey to the one that we expected. You don't need to be alarmed when this happens. Because there are many different paths to the same destination. Be brave and keep heading in a forward direction.

USING ONE DEGREE COURSE CORRECTION

You don't need to make huge changes every day. You only need to use your discipline and be consistent. You might have heard the concept of one-degree course correction. This concept comes from air navigation, which is known as the 1 in 60 rule.

When a plane goes off course, every one degree of difference means it misses its target destination by 1 mile for every 60 miles of flight. So in effect, the further you travel on the wrong course, the further you end up from your destination. Obviously, in air travel, the exact coordinates are essential. Sadly, errors in coordinates by a few degrees can have disastrous results in air travel.

To put this in context, here are some calculations, if the course is one-degree off, so you can see the difference in air travel:

- After one foot, a plane will miss its original target by 0.2 inches.
- After 100 yards, the plane will be wrong by 5.2 feet.
- Once a mile has passed, the plane is 92.2 feet off its destination.
- If you flew around the equator, a one-degree error is 500 miles off course.

So how can this affect you in your life? Well, it can work in two ways:

- One small change or degree can change the trajectory of your life completely. So as mentioned earlier, you might end up on a different path altogether. This is not a bad thing, as it can open up your world to other possibilities.
- You can commit to yourself to do one small (degree) thing every day. Those small things you do over a long time will always accumulate to make a huge difference in your life.

You see, it is important to be consistent, regularly show up, and follow your routines and habits.

However, if you miss something out, don't beat yourself up. It will happen from time to time. All you need to do is get back to it the following day. Push it out of your mind and understand that you are only human. The beauty is, we can always refocus and get ourselves back on track.

Remember, any slight variation in what you are doing can change your path and your results. This is worth bearing in mind if you accidentally do things that are not your normal routines and habits. Don't be surprised if you start feeling and thinking differently from what you originally expected.

ELIMINATING ANALYSIS PARALYSIS

Moving the needle forward, inch by inch is all it takes. These "baby steps" will always add up to a huge leap forward over time. But sometimes, we end up overthinking what we are doing and where we are going. We can end up feeling stuck and suffering from Analysis Paralysis (AP).

We want to move forward, but we overthink so much that we are stuck in the same position.

When you struggle to make decisions and take too much time, you might be experiencing analysis paralysis. You might have a list of things to do, but you think they all have the same level of importance. You can't seem to prioritise them and start to feel bogged down in making the right decisions.

These indecisions then lead on to anxiety as you have still not made any decisions.

It is a pattern that continues, and it can make it hard for you to keep moving forward. It is further complicated if you have goals you want to reach. The goals can feel so much harder than they are in reality.

If you get yourself into such a situation, you can do quite a few things to break these patterns. So you can keep moving that needle forward towards your new life.

Here are some examples:

1. Get Out Of Your Head

Instead of overthinking things in your head, think about how you feel. Start using your gut instincts more to make some decisions. When you have important decisions to make, listen to your body.

- Do you really want to do this new project?

- Does this opportunity feel right for you?

Your gut instinct can help give you the answers and save you precious time. It will stop your brain from imagining every potential scenario and slowing you down.

2. Learn to Prioritise

When you feel anxious, everything feels important. Start to prioritise the things you need to do. It will help to decrease your anxiety and will stop you from procrastinating on everything. A simple, daily to-do list can do wonders to help organise your tasks. It gets the work that needs to be done outside of your head.

3. Practice Making Decisions Quickly

Analysis paralysis slows you down when you want to make decisions and take action. Spin this on its head. Start to make some quick, instant decisions. Instead of mulling over something in your head, make impulsive decisions. Use this system with small things first so that you can gain some confidence. Over time you can move on, making quick decisions for bigger things.

4. Stop Being A Perfectionist

A perfectionist has elements of analysis paralysis rooted in anxiety. Perfectionists want everything to be perfect. They might redo things several times to get it exactly right. This process can waste so much time. If this is you, make a note next time you change an email 10 times, and send it after one check. Feel the real difference.

Overthinking Can Stunt Your Creativity

The effect of analysis paralysis can also affect our creativity. In a study at Stanford University, participants were placed inside fMRI machines and given non-magnetic tablets. The participants were given action words and had to draw several pictures related to these words. They had 30 seconds for each word and had to rank the difficulty for each word picture.

The study found that "the less the participants thought about what they were drawing, the more creative their drawings were." This indicates that overthinking things can lower our creativity. It is valuable research as it shows that thinking too much is not always helpful.

USEFUL TOOLS TO HELP YOU

You might have all your habits, goals, and routines organised. You also might be taking the time to make sure you are on the right course and are not overthinking everything. These are great steps, but many other systems can also help you. Here are a couple of useful ones that will make your journey easier.

Mind Mapping

The actual process of mind mapping is quite therapeutic and a handy tool for your personal development. So what is it? Tony Buzan first used the phrase on BBC's *Use Your Head* program in 1974. It is how we can brainstorm ideas, take notes, and study.

Mind Mapping techniques can help you understand information more clearly. They can also help you be more creative, productive and improve your memory. Mind maps are different from the traditional way that you write down and structure information.

A mind map is when you write down ideas, keywords, and thoughts on a blank canvas.

You use a two-dimensional structure to organise your ideas and write the main idea in the middle. Then you write down related ideas, branching off from the main central idea. These related ideas create a circular structure around the main original idea. There are two different types of mind mapping you can use.

1. The original method Buzan
2. Bubble and Spider Maps

Buzan's mind mapping technique was a system developed after consulting many studies in neuroscience and psychology. The more modern bubble and spider maps use bubbles around the main idea instead of labelling the lines.

Some people prefer the bubble and spider maps as you have more possibilities to link themes.

When you create your own mind map, you can incorporate your habits, routines and goals into it. It helps you have a clear picture of what you are doing in your life. You can create your own using pen and paper or by utilising mind mapping apps.

The Power Of One

The Power of One is an easy system that anybody can use in all areas of their lives. At first, you might think it is only valid for a workplace scenario. However, you can use it in your personal life as well to great effect. It can help you slim down your life and become more focused.

Focus on one day at a time

Keep your focus on the moment. It is better than thinking about the future. Take one day at a time. It will take the pressure off you as you work towards your goal.

Address one piece of communication

If you have 50 emails to handle at work, handle them one at a time. You can still prioritise them, so you don't miss anything urgent. But be strict on looking at only one email. Decide to action it, file it, or reply to it. Don't have multiple emails open at once. You can also use this system with your personal emails.

Move one step forward

No giant leaps forward are needed. We don't want to miss out on the experience of developing. Take your time and move one step forward, never backward.

Read one book

Have you ever read more than one book at a time? It can become a bit of a muddle. Concentrate on reading one book at a time. You will enjoy it more and have a deeper understanding of each one.

You can use the Power of One with anything. It will help you stay focused on what you are doing and will sharpen your self-discipline.

Step One

Look at your daily activities. Find out which task needs to be done straight away and do it.

Step Two

Analyse where you are spending your time and energy. Focus less on future activities and be more focused on your current life.

Step Three

Look at all things and assess if you need to do them now or in the future. If you decide something is not essential and doesn't require immediate attention, you can let it go. You can remove it from your list of things to do and concentrate on the more urgent tasks.

The Power of One is a useful skill to use consistently on our personal development journey. The consistency and focus also help us to use our discipline.

DON'T SWEAT THE SMALL STUFF

You might have heard that title before. It's easy for us to get bothered by simple things in life. But if you can learn to eliminate these frustrations from your life, it can feel quite liberating. If you are a typical "drama king or queen," you probably know what I am referring to.

- Does it matter if you are stuck in a traffic jam?
- Or should you be annoyed if you spill some milk?
- You scratch your sunglasses, and you see it every time you put them on?
- Your work colleague doesn't stop talking, and it gets on your nerves.
- Your small child walks slowly when you have limited time.

Remember, these are all bad habits that you can change.

They are trivial things that are not worth spending your precious energy on. They can affect you in more ways than you probably realize. The next thing you know, you become more stressed and sensitive. Research from the National Institute of Health and Welfare found men under high-stress levels had a reduced lifespan of 2.8 years. It is good to nip any stress in the bud. If you start stressing over little things, they can eventually snowball into bigger things.

Life is not perfect, and neither are we.

If you do have "one of those days," sometimes you have to take it on the chin. There is no point in becoming animated, angry, or annoyed. None of these emotions achieves anything. The best thing you can do is assess the emotion and figure out why you felt like that. It will help you to handle it better next time.

You will then have a higher chance of not reacting negatively.

Another great way to get rid of these annoying things is to put them in the bin literally. The next time something insignificant bothers you, write it on a bit of paper. Then screw it up into a ball and throw it into the bin.

Three Important Points To Remember

Richard Carlson, author of *Don't Sweat the Small Stuff ... and It's All Small Stuff: Simple Ways to Keep the Little Things from Taking over Your Life*, said:

1. Don't procrastinate on relaxing.
2. Give others a break, especially when they don't deserve it.
3. Remember that your life isn't an emergency.

All three of his points are very apt.

- It is important to relax as often as you can. It is essential not to overdo it, or you won't feel like sticking to your routine and habits. You will feel overworked and burnt out. It's not fair on you or the people around you. If you want to be a better version of yourself, you need to start acting like one.
- Don't be quick to overreact if somebody annoys or upsets you. You don't know what is going on in their lives. They might have a hidden illness or other hardships they are dealing with.
- Life is for living. You don't have to think you have to do this and that and please everybody around you. You have to enjoy life and soak it

up. It only happens once, so make sure that you truly throw yourself into it and enjoy it.

INSTANT MAGIC

You can start to add some magic into your life and inch ever closer to the new you. It doesn't matter if you are new to personal development and are not sure where to start. There are simple things you can do to get started right now.

1. Start drinking more water every day. You can start with a glass of water when you wake up, and one before you go to bed at night. Then add one in at lunchtime and so on. Before you know it, you will be drinking more water.
2. Slowly start adding more fruit or vegetables to your regular diet. If you are not a big fan of either, it is important to add the odd thing here or there. Over time, you will get used to it and can start adding more.
3. Make a conscious effort to exercise. Walking is a great way to start doing some form of exercise. It is completely free and can be done anywhere. Start with 10 minutes and gradually build it up.

If you are already doing things like this in your life, think about taking it to the next level.

We can always develop as a person. It doesn't matter how many books or courses we have done. There are always ways to keep improving ourselves. Push yourself further and take action.

CHAPTER EIGHT - ACTION STEP

In Chapter Eight, we have looked at the importance of keeping the needle moving forwards. Enjoying life as much as we can and dealing with issues calmly and rationally can help us progress.

Work your way through the Chapter Eight action steps before you move on to the last chapter.

- Get yourself prepared by creating a "bad day" checklist that you can instantly refer to when it happens. Include the five questions from the first page of this chapter. It will help you dissect your day and avoid any breaks in your routine.
- Avoid analysis paralysis by creating a to-do list. If you haven't already, write your to-do list as part of your night routine, so you're all set for the following day.

- Think of a little thing you can do to add some extra magic into your life. For example, drink 6 glasses of water. Eat one piece of fruit. Start doing it and stick to it.

MAGIC MINDSET

"Self-discipline is the magic power that makes you virtually unstoppable."

— DAN KENNEDY

This chapter is the last one of the book. But by no means is it the end of your journey with discipline. Self-discipline is a muscle that needs daily use. Over time it can gain strength and will continue to push you to more incredible things in your life. So you can stay curious, open, and ready to embark on new opportunities when they arise.

Discipline can help you to maintain a *growth mindset* throughout your life.

Reading this book has helped to plant your development seeds. Or if you were already growing your inner personal development plant. It can nurture it as it grows. Your self-discipline is the secret to achieving success in your life.

FIXED MINDSET VS GROWTH MINDSET

Carol Dweck, a Professor of Psychology at Stanford University, was the first to talk about growth and fixed mindsets. Her book, *Mindset: The New Psychology of Success* discussed implicit theories connected to intelligence.

Professor Dweck recognised two different mindsets: a fixed mindset and a growth mindset. After the book's release in 2006, she went on to give several fascinating talks about mindset.

So what is the difference between a fixed and growth mindset?

The differences are very distinct. Your mindset group depends on your views regarding ability or intelligence. These two mindsets play a huge role in all aspects of someone's life. Here are the main differences between the two different types of mindset:

Fixed Mindset

People who have a fixed mindset have a "fixed" view of their intelligence. It is hard to sway them from their thoughts.

- They believe that all their success happens because of their natural ability.
- Fixed mindset people have the same view on their intelligence and talents.
- Their mission is always to look clever and never look stupid.

Growth Mindset

People with a growth mindset tend to have polar opposite views. They have a "growth" theory on intelligence.

- They believe their success is related to hard work, learning, self-discipline, and training.
- Growth mindset people understand that abilities and talents can develop through effort, persistence, and good teaching.
- They don't believe everybody has the same intelligence or can be Einstein. But realise everyone can get smarter if they work hard.

The Good And The Bad

You might not be aware of your current mindset, but your behaviour indicates your mindset. You will find that people with a fixed mindset are scared of failure. They view it as a negative statement of their abilities. On the other hand, people with a growth mindset don't fear failure as much. They view it as a pure learning process and realise their performance has to improve.

Dweck believes a growth mindset is best because people can have less stress and more success in their lives.

FIXED MINDSET + DISCIPLINE = STUCK IN YOUR WAYS

The equation in the title is a quick way to show how a fixed mindset and discipline are not friends. They don't work well together and can sometimes make you feel even more stuck in your ways.

People with a fixed mindset truly believe their traits are permanent and cannot be changed.

It doesn't matter if they try to use their discipline. If people persist with a fixed mindset, they will never reach their goals. They don't comprehend that successful people will have worked hard to get there.

Very few people reach their goals without doing any hard work.

A fixed mindset is completely closed to determination, hard work, persistence, trial and error. Sadly, all these things relate to using your self-discipline. It's not all doom and gloom, though. If you have fixed mindset traits, it is possible to change them.

It would help if you were brutally honest with yourself. This introspection allows you to become self-aware of your fixed traits. You can then tell yourself that you need to change these traits.

GROWTH MINDSET + DISCIPLINE = A MAGICAL LIFE

You have read about the limitations of a fixed mindset. But imagine the unique possibilities you have with a growth mindset. A growth mindset helps to power up your self-discipline. It makes you aware of your mistakes and any restrictions you have placed on yourself. The critical difference is that you know you can change the results.

You set out to educate yourself and learn how to improve yourself.

You are comfortable with the fact that it might take some time and hard work to get there. But you know that you will reach your goals and show up every day to achieve them. No dream is too big for you. You like the challenge and learning from your failures.

USE THE RIGHT MINDSET

Taking all this into account, you can see that your life will only be as good as your mindset. Ideally, we should all strive to have a growth mindset. Of course, there will be times when we have a fixed perspective on certain things. The trick is to recognise these selected thoughts and actions and change them into growth ones.

THE POWER OF A GROWTH MINDSET

It is important to remember what discipline means in our lives. It doesn't have to be strict and uncomfortable. It is an inner device we all have naturally inside of us that can keep us moving forward. If you view it as a push to your goals, some people may feel discomfort. But if you change this around and view it as a pull towards your goals, it might feel more comfortable.

It's like having that special friend that is encouraging you along the way.

Professor Dweck, meanwhile, continues her groundbreaking research into mindsets. A National Study of Learning Mindset in 2019 tried growth mindset intervention on maths students. Dweck and her behavioural science peers wanted to see if growth mindset interventions could improve students' academic performances.

They conducted short (less than an hour) online interventions. The students learnt that they could develop their intellectual abilities over time. The interventions managed to improve grades among the students that were lower-achievers. It also helped to increase enrollment in advanced maths courses nationally.

MAGIC MINDSET IDEAS

A growth mindset, coupled with your discipline, can create magical results. It is worth looking into ways to cultivate your discipline and make it even more powerful. Self-discipline is the bridge between your goals and accomplishing them. Here are some ideas to help you create your magic:

1. Use Implementation Intentions

Problems will arise along the way. You will have already planned for this as much as you can. You have your habits, intentions, and routines to help you. But sometimes, things happen in life that can knock you sideways. These moments are dangerous as you might be inclined to give up. Not because you want to, but because you don't know what to do.

It's like the proverbial curveball that hits you smack in the face.

So, what can you do to get around these situations? Well, the answer is to create some implementation intentions. According to scientific research published in Science Direct, <u>94 independent studies found that implementation intentions positively affected attaining goals.</u> They are a bit like habits on steroids. They can help you to get going, protect you against distractions and repeated negative behaviour. It works like this:

- The original goal intention was - "I intend to reach Z!"
- The new implementation intention is - "If situation Y is encountered, then I will initiate (goal-directed behaviour) X!"

As you can see, you can use implementation intention for any potential bad situation related to your goals. It's like having a backup plan to protect you from giving up. It is another valuable tool to put in your back pocket, in case you need it. Here are some practical examples:

- "If I get up early in the morning, I will instantly go for a walk!"

- "If I don't feel like doing something, I will do it anyway!"
- "If I feel like resetting my alarm in the morning, I will instantly get out of bed!"

2. Excuse Bashing

Excuses are those little moments that appear in your life and challenge you. When you come across an excuse in your life to do something, you need to challenge it back. A slight change in your mindset can tackle these excuses and keep you going. Some good examples would be:-

- "I can't do any exercise because I don't have a gym membership." You can go for a walk outside or find an exercise video on YouTube and do that at home.
- "I don't have enough hours in the day to manage my blog as well as my job." You can get up earlier in the morning and set time aside to write your blog.
- "I don't have enough money to buy the course I want to do." You can get a second job in the evening or a weekend job. Then use your discipline to save the money needed, to buy the course you want.

3. Measure Your Progress

I touched on this earlier in the book, but you need to measure your progress to improve yourself. It is also a neat way to keep your mindset positive and focused. In our modern world, it is possible to monitor practically anything. Here are a few examples:

- Use a smartphone, pedometer, or Fitbit, to track your steps.
- Use a budget app to monitor your money or a simple excel spreadsheet.
- Use weighing scales at the chemist or in your home.
- Use a time management tracking app or a Pomodoro timer.
- Or simply a notepad and pen.

When you have a tracking system in place, it is easier for you to see how you are doing. It can also help to see your progress over time and helps to increase your self-discipline.

4. Tackle The Big Things First

To-do lists are great and can help you to prioritize your work and personal chores. But sometimes, even prioritizing can get a bit challenging. Sometimes when we have these vast tasks to do, it might seem a little daunting.

You can get around this by using the advice from Mark Twain's famous quote.

"If it's your job to eat a frog, it's best to do it first thing in the morning. If it's your job to eat two frogs, it's best to eat the biggest one first."

If you follow this advice, before you know it, you will have done that mammoth task. The rest of the tasks and your day will feel more enjoyable and achievable. It is because you have eliminated any potential stressful deadline by completing the most challenging task first.

5. You Are Your Boss

Sometimes you might feel a little hesitant to go ahead and do things, especially if you are stepping outside of your comfort bubble. You might think that you need "permission" from somebody you know. You don't. Take ownership of your actions and decisions. It will make you feel stronger in your mind and sharpen your self-discipline. Learn to trust yourself.

Don't worry about what people think about you.

You don't need permission to do things, as you are creating a better version of yourself. It is for you. However, the knock-on effects can also be fantastic, as those who know and love you will also love the new you. Take charge of your life and enjoy the positive changes that will come to you.

4. Keep It Clean

A cluttered mind can't think straight, but a clean one can. Your immediate surroundings can affect the way you think. Therefore, make a special effort to keep your desk at work, your home surroundings, your car, etc., clean.

Because it's not just keeping the place clean that can help but the actual act of decluttering. In Psychology Today, Alice Boyes. PhD discussed the psychological benefits of decluttering your space.

Here are the main points to inspire you to give it a go:

- When things start feeling like hard work, you can take a break and do some decluttering in the middle of a project or task. It can give your mind a break and the space to receive insightful ideas. Also, the physical effort spent decluttering is also beneficial for your overall health.

- Decluttering can decrease potential stress with other colleagues or family members. They will respect what you have done and why and make sure to maintain a clean environment.
- Decluttering is excellent for your self-discipline and confidence. You will only have a limited amount of space to organise everything. It makes you focus on where to put things and how. Also, you have to make decisions to throw some things away. When you have completed the task, it can bolster your confidence and feelings of satisfaction.

ENJOY SCARY GOALS

You can let your discipline push or pull you, whatever works best for you. You can also consider doing things that scare you.

These could end up being real breakthroughs in your life.

As Eleanor Roosevelt said, *"You must do the thing you think you cannot do."* So, how can you get your head around tackling these exciting but scary goals?

- Start it. Get yourself ready, and give it a go. You will never know if it is right for you unless you try it.
- Meditate on it. Think about why the goal seems scary to you. This exercise is a great mechanism to figure out what is going on inside of you. You might realise it is the same thing holding you back in other areas of your life.
- Visualise the endgame. How will you feel when you achieve this scary goal? Reminding yourself of the result could be the last push or pull you need.
- Look for other hidden benefits. If you complete this goal, are there other benefits to you? For example: Can it help you get a promotion at

work? Can you increase your social circle? Can it make you feel healthier?

Once you have completed one of your "scary goals", you can look back and be amazed. You did it, nobody else. It can help to boost your self-discipline and improve your mindset. Let's face it if you can do that. You can do anything.

BECOME A FORWARD THINKER

This book has given you some great ideas to harness your self-discipline so it can work for you. However, some people like to push the boundaries even further and think outside the box. If this sounds like you, you are probably a "forward thinker".

The good news is, everybody can think in this way.

The same way as you use your self-discipline with a growth mindset. You can learn to think ahead of the game like the best visionaries. Like Marcus Aurelius famously said,

---

"You have power over your mind—not outside events. Realise this, and you will find strength."

— MARCUS AURELIUS

1. It is an understanding that you are responsible for your destiny. So, making your own decisions without asking for advice and realising the Law of Cause and Effect. You can create the life that you want if you think outside the box.
2. Become open to all possibilities. Things will change, and so will you as you grow in the process. Therefore, if somebody or some situation presents you with an alternative solution, you are open to it. You don't dismiss it because it is not part of "your plan". You learn to adapt to different situations.
3. Visualising what your life and you will look like in the future. It can make it feel more natural on those days when you feel like you are stuck in the mud. It reminds you of the ultimate destination.
4. By nature, most people are either analytical or creative. But it is possible to use both of these skills. Search for the sweet point, so you use both and balance the two. This skillset will make you a force to be reckoned with and can propel your forward-thinking into greatness.

5. Forward thinkers, as you would expect, do not think about the past. They deliberately focus on what they are doing right now and where it will take them. So, whatever issues or problems they had in the past does not affect them in the slightest.
6. Forward thinkers keep an eye on the larger picture. They don't sweat the small stuff and know that everything is connected. This understanding enables them to deal with unforeseen things, after all, it's all part of the whole picture.

RESPECTING YOURSELF

"Respect your efforts, respect yourself. Self-respect leads to self-discipline. When you have both firmly under your belt, that's real power."

— CLINT EASTWOOD

On your self-discipline journey, you will learn a lot about yourself. It would be best if you respect yourself and your efforts. Be gentle with yourself as you learn and grow. You might have to eliminate some things from your life that you have done for years. Shedding things might feel hard. But it is all part and parcel of growing as a person.

Take The Emotion Out Of It

Once you know more about yourself, you will understand why you react in specific ways. Your self-discipline will help you to handle criticism in a more wholesome way. You can take the comments on board and process them.

If the criticism is not constructive, you will feel comfortable asking for further clarification. In the past, you might have buried your head in the sand or worried about what you did wrong. Now, you want to know more so you can continue evolving.

Expect Respect

Expect respect from everybody that you know and treat everybody with respect. You don't need to associate with people or situations that give you no respect. Choose to be around positive and friendly people, and you will enjoy the warmth of genuine care. Go where you are celebrated, not where you are tolerated.

Divine Discipline

Every day, when you chose to be disciplined and stick to your habits, processes, routines, and goals. You are respecting yourself and your beliefs. You are following your path to a better version of yourself and a more fulfilling life.

Discipline creates even more discipline, and so it grows in your life.

Plus, on those days when you do fail, it isn't a failure. With your growth mindset, you can handle these situations with ease. You already respect yourself enough to know that you can get back up, dust yourself off, and continue on your path to success.

CHAPTER NINE - ACTION STEP

You will now understand how influential your mindset can be in your life. You can also make a distinction between the two different mindsets. You learnt more about the benefits of pushing yourself and respecting yourself in the development process.

These are your final action steps in the book.

- Write down a list of your growth and fixed mindset traits. Pick a fixed mindset from your list and vow to change this thought process. Create a habit that will help you do this.
- Think about a goal that deep down you would love to do but have been too scared to set. Set it and embrace the feeling of learning something new.
- Create three implementation intentions to help you achieve your goals.

CONCLUSION

"I've learned life is a lot like surfing. When you get caught in the impact zone, you need to get right back up, because you never know what's over the next wave......and if you have faith, anything is possible, anything at all."

— BETHANY HAMILTON (SOUL SURFER)

Developing yourself takes time, dedication, and above all, discipline. Before you read this book, you might have thought you knew the ins and outs of discipline. However, you will have since discovered that discipline is an incredibly versatile inner tool. The real bonus is, we can all use it to better our lives.

It doesn't matter at what stage you are in your personal development. The action steps and examples in this book apply to everybody.

People who want to learn more about themselves and start to create a more fulfilling life. Also, people already on their development journey, wanting to take it to the next level. Everything is possible if you can use your self-discipline to help you. It enables you to demand the highest standards from yourself and maintain them.

Loving yourself and showing yourself self-respect will also help you to build your self-discipline. Self-care is powerful. It can help you to assess and reassess your life gently. Monitor your results and adjust your system as you go along. You can then fine-tune your self-discipline to make it work in the best way for you.

The quote from Bethany Hamilton resonates with us all. Our lives are full of so many waves, and learning to handle them takes time. This is where your self-discipline can shine through as you set out on your path of development. You can learn to handle the waves.

You can start changing the challenges in your life and make them your opportunities.

In Bethany's case, she lost an arm in a shark attack while surfing. But instead of letting this traumatic event affect her confidence and self-esteem. She used her self-discipline to keep going. Her disability has not deterred her, and she keeps moving forward to create the life she wants.

You can use the same mental toughness to create freedom and the best life for yourself.

Don't be scared of failure, and don't let a bad day put you off. You can learn from your failures and forget about those bad days. Eating that tub of ice-cream, missing a day of your online course, or forgetting to exercise is not the end of the world. These things are sent to test us, and your discipline can help you get back on track.

Discipline is one of the most important ingredients in the recipe for success. It is often overlooked, and "easier" elements are discussed in personal development. But do yourself the biggest favour by nurturing and increasing your self-discipline. It is the best foundation stone you can have to create your new best life.

TRANSFORMING YOURSELF

So you can facilitate the real change that you want in your life. Work your way slowly through this book and carefully implement the action steps along the way. Think about the times when you have read self-help books and then moved on to read the next one. Break this habit, make a promise that **you will use this book to help you transform yourself.**

I also recommend that you **re-read this book again in 3 months** and occasionally thereafter. Doing this will further help you instil discipline into your life. It will be a regular reminder, so you can keep going and avoid any of the pitfalls. The better version of yourself will be eternally grateful that you have made this extra effort.

KEY TAKEAWAYS

Here are the book's key takeaways from each chapter, so you can remember what areas you need to focus on. Note that these takeaways are a summary. So if you need further clarification, it is best to go back and reread that particular chapter.

What Is Discipline?

- Discipline is doing things we don't want to do, but we know we should anyway. It gives you the power of self-control, which you can use in all areas of your life.
- Anybody can use discipline in their lives. It helps you to see that failures are learning blocks. You can use your inner self-control to help you stay the course.
- It is like having a superpower, which you can use to gain freedom in your life. You can stick to your plans and keep going till you reach your goals.

The Difference Between Motivation And Discipline

- Discipline is completely different from motivation. Motivation helps you in the short-term. But discipline keeps you going long-term until you achieve success.
- Motivation is heavily connected to your emotions. Discipline, on the other hand, has nothing to do with emotion. It is a systematic process that you need to follow.
- Self-discipline works best when you "throw yourself into it" and believe in the process. You know, deep down, that if you follow the system, it will work for you.

Creating A Healthy Body

- It is important to look after your body by eating healthy meals and exercising. You might look great on the outside, but inside you might have health issues.
- When you want to become the best version of yourself, you need to treat your body with respect. What you put inside can affect how you are on the outside.
- It is best to eat food with high, positive vibrational energy instead of unhealthy

processed food. When in doubt, choose the healthier option.

Protecting Your Mental Health

- It is important to look after your mental health so that you can feel mentally fit. This will have a knock-on effect and enhance your body and mind connection.
- You can use meditation, mindfulness, and urge surfing techniques. They can all help to alleviate stress and build up your discipline.
- Discipline can give you mental clarity. It helps by making you think first before you make any impulsive actions and decisions. You can learn from any mistakes.

The Benefits Of Habit Creation

- You can use a habit loop to write over your bad habits and create good ones. Setting up new routines and creating better habits can improve your productivity.
- New habits help you break out of your comfort bubble and experience new things. The habits can help to broaden your horizons and increase your self-discipline.

- You can start to eliminate triggers from your life. You can also control your urges using timed interval training. Over time you will use discipline on auto-pilot.

How The Compound Effect Works

- The compound effect is a long-term strategy that converts small, consistent actions into major gains in your life. You can use it in all areas of your life.
- The Law of Cause and Effect dictates that you will receive a similar consequence for every action. So always make positive actions and decisions in your life.
- The Chinese Bamboo Tree parable shows it takes time for your efforts to show fruition. But you need to stick with the process till you see the results.

Enjoy The Valentine's Day Feeling

- It is important to retain a happy and positive attitude. The Law of Attraction dictates that you ultimately attract what "you send out". So make it positive!

- A slow, steady approach to reaching your goals is far more rewarding. It helps to enjoy the process and notice the changes in you instead of rushing to the end.
- Don't be afraid of any challenges and obstacles when they appear in your life. You can use them to your advantage, learn from them, and over time enjoy them.

Managing Your Momentum

- It is important to keep moving forward every day. Even a small step forward helps to keep the momentum flowing as you move further towards your goal.
- Don't be scared to make any decisions. You can become more decisive in your life. It can help you to stop paralysis analysis and eliminate stress.
- You can use mind mapping. Also, The Power of One system. These tools can help you stay organised and create space for forward-thinking.

Using The Best Mindset

- A growth mindset helps to keep you focused. You accept failures as learning moments in your life. You understand that it takes time to achieve your goals.
- You can create more discipline by using implementation intentions. They can protect you from distractions and repeating negative behaviour traits.
- Don't worry about the small things in life. Bad days will happen, but how you deal with them

makes the difference. Stay positive and focused on your goals.

FINAL THOUGHTS

The takeaways above are a great reminder of the many valuable skills you will learn. The overall process to reach your goals will take time, but it is 100% worth it. Your inner discipline will be there for you. It can help you to get to where you want to be. You only need to believe in the system and follow it, and it will believe in you.

Already, by promising yourself to work on this book's action steps, you have started using your self-discipline.

When your self-discipline develops further, you will find other positive influences will appear. These positive influences will carry over into all areas of your life:

1. You will be more ready to take responsibility for things in your life.
2. You will live more in the moment so that you can help yourself and others.
3. Your time management will be second to none. Always early and never late.

4. Breaks will become as important as working, and you will enjoy both equally.
5. People will feel inspired by your attitude and the way you conduct yourself.

Don't let anything stand in your way to success.

The world truly is your oyster, and you can finally achieve your brightest dreams and desires. Don't forget that the journey is also as rewarding as the destination. Remember to enjoy the little "wins" along the way and learn from your failures. You can also use your new skills and your powerhouse discipline to live your best life.

You are now ready to start creating the life that you want. As Napoleon Hill said,

---

"Don't wait. The time will never be just right. Start where you stand, and work whatever tools you may have at your command, and better tools will be found as you go along."

Go out there and give it all you've got. You don't have to wait till next Monday, next month, or next year. You can start working on it straight away. You can use your magical discipline to gain freedom and become the best version of yourself. Enjoy every minute!

SPREAD THE WORD

If you enjoyed this book, I would appreciate it if you could take a few moments to **leave a review on Amazon.** Your review could make a positive difference in somebody's life. They, too, can learn about the magic of discipline and how to use it to improve themselves. Your caring and sharing attitude can help make the world a better place.

Let's Connect

Feel free to drop me a line and say hello at: contact@nmhill.com

REFERENCES

CHAPTER ONE

CCMS Editor. (2017b, April 20). Carleton Study Finds People Spending a Third of Job Time on Email. Carleton Newsroom Archives. Retrieved 17 October 2022, from https://newsroom.carleton.ca/archives/2017/04/20/carleton-study-finds-people-spending-third-job-time-email/

Gatz, M. G. (2021, January 4). Childhood self-control forecasts the pace of midlife aging and preparedness for old age. PNAS. https://www.pnas.org/doi/10.1073/pnas.2010211118

Sasson, R. (n.d.). What Is Self-Discipline – Definitions and Meaning. Success Consciousness. https://www.

successconsciousness.com/blog/inner-strength/what-is-self-discipline

Self Discipline: Its Benefits and Importance (Sport & Life). (2018, May 12). Triathlon Lab. https://triathlonlab.com/blogs/news/self-discipline-its-benefits-and-importance-sport-life#:~:text=Self%20discipline%20gives%20you%20the,important%20requirements%20-for%20achieving%20goals.&text=This%20ability%20leads%20to%20to,consequently%20to%20happiness%20and%20satisfaction

CHAPTER TWO

Motivation vs discipline: the Yin and Yang of health | Second Nature Guides. (n.d.). Second Nature. Retrieved 17 October 2022, from https://www.secondnature.io/nl/guides/mind/motivation/+motivation-vs-discipline

Intrinsic vs extrinsic motivation | Second Nature Guides. (n.d.). Second Nature. Retrieved 17 October 2022, from https://www.secondnature.io/nl/guides/mind/motivation/+intrinsic-vs-extrinsic-motivation

What Is Extrinsic Motivation and Is It Effective? (2018, September 18). Healthline. https://www.healthline.com/health/extrinsic-motivation

BusinessMirror. (2017, September 21). Motivation vs Self-Discipline: Which Is the Key to Habit Formation? - BusinessMirror. BusinessMirror - a Broader Look at Today's Business. Retrieved 17 October 2022, from https://businessmirror.com.ph/2017/09/21/motivation-vs-+self-discipline-which-is-the-key-to-habit-formation/

Odanga, S. O. (2018, July). Strategies for Increasing Students' Self-motivation. Research Gate. https://www.researchgate.net/publication/326556176_Strategies_for_Increasing_Students'_Self-motivation

Villarica, H. V. (2012, April 12). The Chocolate-and-Radish Experiment That Birthed the Modern Conception of Willpower. The Atlantic. https://www.theatlantic.com/health/archive/2012/04/the-chocolate-and-radish-experiment-that-birthed-the-modern-conception-of-willpower/255544/

Ego Depletion: Is the Active Self a Limited Resource? (1997, June 16). http://faculty.washington.edu/jdb/345/345%20Articles/Baumeister%20et%20al.%20%281998%29.pdf

Inzlicht, M. I., & Friese, M. F. (2019, November 5). The Past, Present, and Future of Ego Depletion. Hogrefe Econtent. https://econtent.hogrefe.com/doi/full/10.1027/1864-9335/a000398

CHAPTER THREE

https://daylekinney.com/2017/07/19/19-july-what-goes-in-must-come-out/

Branson, R. B. (2019, June 24). The importance of being healthy. Virgin. https://www.virgin.com/branson-family/richard-branson-blog/the-importance-of-being-healthy

Sasson, R. S. (n.d.). 9 Reasons Why Self-Discipline Is Good for Your Health. Success Consciousness.

Tips On How To Be More Disciplined About Your Health. (2020, June 6). Health Works Collective. Retrieved 17 October 2022, from https://www.healthworkscollective.com/tips-on-how-to-be-+more-disciplined-about-your-health/

Obesity and overweight. (2021, June 9). World Health Organisation. https://www.who.int/news-room/fact-sheets/detail/obesity-and-overweight

Lin, X. (2020, September 8). Global, regional, and national burden and trend of diabetes in 195 countries and territories: an analysis from 1990 to 2025. Nature. Retrieved 17 October 2022, from https://www.nature.com/articles/s41598-020-71908-9?error=

cookies_not_supported&code=cedbdb6c-c302-4b32-b333-b0a796124c7f

Gibson, K. (2020, August 4). Mastering Self-Discipline to Improve your Health. Nutrition Innovated. Retrieved 17 October 2022, from https://www.nutritioninnovated.co.za/blog/lifestyle-nutrition/mastering-self-discipline-to-improve-your-health/

Elease, K. E. (2020, June 14). Self-Discipline: Benefits for Your Health. Kayla Elease. https://kaylaelease.com/posts/2020/1/20/self-discipline-benefits-for-your-health

Vibrational Food. (n.d.). Nutrition. Retrieved 17 October 2022, from https://healthcenternutrition.webs.com/vibrationalfood.htm

CHAPTER FOUR

Team, S. (2022, February 15). Mental health statistics 2022. The Checkup. Retrieved 17 October 2022, from https://www.singlecare.com/blog/news/mental-health-+statistics/

10 Ways of Journaling Your Way to Better Goals in Your Life. (2021, January 27). Verywell Mind. Retrieved 17 October 2022, from https://www.verywellmind.com/goal-setting-strategies-for-stress-relief-3144671

404 - Stripes. (n.d.). Stars and Stripes. Retrieved 17 October 2022, from https://www.stripes.com/theaters/us/army-tests-fitness-benefits-+of-yoga-and-meditation-in-basic-training-1.663284

Rosen, D. A. R. (n.d.). How Meditation Benefits Mental Health. The Center for Treatment of Anxiety and Mood Disorders. https://centerforanxietydisorders.com/how-meditation- benefits-mental-health/

Gibson-Judkins, C. L. (2019, November 8). How Active Meditation Can Boost Your Mental Health. Eggleston Youth Center. Retrieved 17 October 2022, from https://www.egglestonyouthcenter.org/blog/active-+meditation-for-improved-mental-and-physical-health/

How Meditation Builds Self Control, Willpower, Discipline – EOC Institute. (n.d.). Retrieved 17 October 2022, from https://eocinstitute.org/meditation/boosting-willpower-self-+discipline/

Consumer Health. (2022, October 11). Mayo Clinic. https://www.mayoclinic.org/healthy-lifestyle/consumer- health/in-depth/mindfulness-exercises/art-20046356

What Is Mindfulness? (n.d.). Taking Charge of Your Health & Wellbeing. Retrieved 17 October 2022, from https://www.takingcharge.csh.umn.edu/what-mindfulness

Cosmic Media LLC. (2022, July 8). What Is The Law Of Attraction & How Does It Work? The Law of Attraction. Retrieved 17 October 2022, from https://thelawofattraction.com/what-is-the-law-of-+attraction/

Northey, J. M. (2018, February 1). Exercise interventions for cognitive function in adults older than 50: a systematic review with meta-analysis. British Journal of Sports Medicine. Retrieved 17 October 2022, from https://bjsm.bmj.com/content/52/3/154

NCBI - WWW Error Blocked Diagnostic. (n.d.-b). Retrieved 17 October 2022, from https://pubmed.ncbi.nlm.nih.gov/29361921/

CHAPTER FIVE

West, M. (n.d.). 5 Reasons Why It's Important to Develop Good Habits. Retrieved 17 October 2022, from https://thriveglobal.com/stories/5-reasons-why-its-important-+to-develop-good-habits/

The importance of good habits. (n.d.). The World Counts. https://www.theworldcounts.com/happiness/the-importance- of-good-habits

Dartmouth College. (2020, February 27). Revving habits up and down, new insight into how the brain forms habits. ScienceDaily. Retrieved October 17, 2022 from www.sciencedaily.com/releases/2020/02/200227144230.htm

Williams, C. (2019, March 31). The Importance Of Habits: 5 ways to actually stick with them. Zephyr Cycling Studio. Retrieved 17 October 2022, from https://zephyrcyclingstudio.com/2019/01/18/the-importance-+of-habits/

Cressy, G. S. I. (n.d.). The (Super) Power of Habits and Routines. Grotto. https://grottonetwork.com/navigate-life/career-and-finance/why-habits-are-important/

Gardner, B. G., Lally, P. L., & Wardle, J. W. (n.d.). Making health habitual: the psychology of 'habit-formation' and general practice. National Library of Medicine. https://www.ncbi.nlm.nih.gov/pmc/articles/PMC3505409/

Daily, T. A. (2016, January 25). 7 Reasons Why It Is Important to Form Good Habits and How to Do It. The Alternative Daily. Retrieved 17 October 2022, from https://www.thealternativedaily.com/the-importance-of-good-+habits/

A Guide to Developing the Self-Discipline Habit. (2022, April 18). Zen Habits. Retrieved 17 October 2022, from https://zenhabits.net/self-discipline/

Castrillon, C. C. (2020, December 13). https://www.forbes.com/sites/carolinecastrillon/2020/12/13/ 5-morning-habits-of-highly-successful-people/? sh=47fcdb685ec6. Forbes. https://www.forbes.com/sites/carolinecastrillon/2020/12/13/ 5-morning-habits-of-highly-successful-people/? sh=47fcdb685ec6

Arthur, R. (2018, January 18). The Morning Holy Hour. Neil Strauss. Retrieved 17 October 2022, from https://www.neilstrauss.com/advice/the-morning-holy-hour/

Edwards, V. van. (2022, June 17). Perfect Your Morning Routine With 10 Research Backed Steps. Science of People. Retrieved 17 October 2022, from https://www.scienceofpeople.com/morning-routine/

How to develop self discipline. (n.d.). Headspace. https://www.headspace.com/blog/2017/10/16/resist-temptation-build-self-discipline/

Arthur, R. (2018b, April 24). How to Sleep Like A Boss. Neil Strauss. Retrieved 17 October 2022, from https://www.neilstrauss.com/advice/how-to-sleep-like-a-boss/

CHAPTER SIX

Yu, A. (2015, June 7). A Penny Doubled Everyday. Alan Yu Business and Finance Blog. Retrieved 17 October

2022, from https://www.al6400.com/blog/a-penny-doubled-everyday/

Farrington, R. (2022, September 29). Would You Rather Have A Penny That Doubles Each Day For A Month Or $1 Million? The College Investor. Retrieved 17 October 2022, from https://thecollegeinvestor.com/17145/would-you-rather-have-+a-penny-that-doubles-each-day-for-a-month-or-1-million/

The Compound Effect. (2012, January 23). Leadership Now. https://www.leadershipnow.com/leadingblog/2012/01/the_compound_effect.html

Fox, M. (2022, September 13). What Is The Law of Cause and Effect – 12 Universal Laws Explained. SelfMadeLadies. Retrieved 17 October 2022, from https://selfmadeladies.com/universal-laws-cause-effect/

7 Tips From the Compound Effect That Will Make You Successful. (n.d.). Great Performers. https://greatperformersacademy.com/books/7-tips-from-the-compound-effect-that-will-make-you-successful

Gowrie, K. (2020, March 28). 5 THINGS WE LEARNED FROM THE COMPOUND EFFECT. Yes Supply TM. Retrieved 17 October 2022, from https://www.yessupply.co/5-things-learned-compound-effect/

atma. (2018, July 8). The Chinese Bamboo Tree - Les Brown. YouTube. Retrieved 17 October 2022, from https://www.youtube.com/watch?v=0e1LYMhgxTk

The Story of The Chinese Bamboo Tree - Women's Network Australia. (2020, January 29). Women's Network Australia. Retrieved 17 October 2022, from https://www.womensnetwork.com.au/the-story-of-the-+chinese-bamboo-tree/

CHAPTER 7

Copquin, C. G. (2013, February 5). Life Is What Happens While We're Not Checking Facts. HuffPost. Retrieved 17 October 2022, from https://www.huffpost.com/entry/gilda-radner_b_2231040

Shippers, M. C. S., Morisano, D. M., Locke, E. A. L., Scheepers, A. W. A. S., Latham, G. P. L., & De Jong, E. M. D. (2019, November 25). Writing about personal goals and plans regardless of goal type boosts academic performance. Science Direct. https://www.sciencedirect.com/science/article/pii/S0361476X1930428X#!

Kaplan, E. K. (2018, May 3). MONEY 7 ways to increase your success and enjoy the process. CNBC. https://www.cnbc.com/2018/05/03/ceo-elle-kaplan-

7-ways-to-increase-success-while-enjoying-the-process.html

Manninen, S. (2017, June 21). Social Laughter Triggers Endogenous Opioid Release in Humans. Journal of Neuroscience. Retrieved 17 October 2022, from https://www.jneurosci.org/content/37/25/6125

Clifton, B. J. (2022, August 4). The World's Broken Workplace. Gallup.com. Retrieved 17 October 2022, from https://news.gallup.com/opinion/chairman/212045/world-+broken-workplace.aspx?g_source=position1

Ressem, J. (2018, June 14). To Fall In Love With The Process - Jonas Ressem. Medium. Retrieved 17 October 2022, from https://jonasressem.medium.com/to-fall-in-love-with-the-process-aaf27db6f42c

Kyle, K. (2021, January 26). 10 Goal Setting Statistics: Research Studies Facts & Findings. Kath Kyle. Retrieved 17 October 2022, from https://www.kathkyle.com/goal-setting-statistics/

Matthews, G. M. (n.d.). / GOALS RESEARCH SUMMARY. Boost Profits. https://boostprofits.com/wp-content/uploads/Goals-Research-Summary.pdf?x60870

Byers, T. B. (2022, May 2). The Power of the Mind Through Visualization. Swimming World. https://www.swimmingworldmagazine.com/news/the-power-of-the-mind-through-visualization/

The Relationship Between Self Discipline and Self Esteem | NeilSchwartz.net. (n.d.). Retrieved 17 October 2022, from https://www.neilschwartz.net/the-relationship-between-self-+discipline-and-self-esteem/

Logan, T., & Logan, T. (n.d.). Falling In Love With The Process, Not The Results. Conscious Magazine. Retrieved 17 October 2022, from https://consciousmagazine.co/falling-in-love-with-the-+process-not-the-results/

Hamilton, B. (2021, November 22). Trusting the Process: 10 Reasons We Should Enjoy the Journey and Stop Worrying About the Outcome. Breaking Muscle. Retrieved 17 October 2022, from https://breakingmuscle.com/trusting-the-process-10-reasons-we-should-enjoy-the-journey-and-stop-worrying-about-the-outc/

Enjoying the process, not just the result. (2018, August 9). Club Gym Wellness. Retrieved 17 October 2022, from https://www.clubgymwellness.co.uk/enjoying-the-process-not-just-+the-result/

Smith, L. C. (2015, March 11). Thriving Is All About Enjoying the Process Purposefully. HuffPost. Retrieved 17 October 2022, from https://www.huffpost.com/entry/thriving-is-all-about-enjoying-the-process-purposefully_b_6439280mindbodygreen.

(2022, September 21). Are You An Achievement Junkie? Here's How To Enjoy The Process. Mindbodygreen. Retrieved 17 October 2022, from https://www.mindbodygreen.com/articles/ways-to-enjoy-the-process-as-much-as-the-achievement

CHAPTER EIGHT

Tandem Financial | The power of one degree course correction. (n.d.). Retrieved 17 October 2022, from https://tandemfinancial.co.uk/tandem-thinking/the-power-of-+one-degree-course-correction/

Taibbi, R. T. (2019, April 24). Do You Have Analysis Paralysis? Psychology Today. https://www.psychologytoday.com/us/blog/fixing-families/201904/do-you-have-analysis-paralysis

Raypole, C. (2020, April 27). How to Beat 'Analysis Paralysis' and Make All the Decisions. Healthline. Retrieved 17 October 2022, from https://www.healthline.com/health/mental-health/analysis-paralysis

Johnson, E. B. (2021, December 9). How to stop overthinking - Practical Growth. Medium. Retrieved 17 October 2022, from https://medium.com/practical-growth/stop-overthinking-6e505ea9aba3

Schmerler, J. S. (2015, May 28). Don't Overthink It, Less Is More When It Comes to Creativity. Scientific American. https://www.scientificamerican.com/article/don-t-overthink-it-less-is-more-when-it-comes-to-creativity/

Brandner, R. (2021, April 23). Why Mind Mapping Is So Powerful and How It Works | FOCUS. Focus. Retrieved 17 October 2022, from https://www.mindmeister.com/blog/why-mind-mapping/

Scudder, J. A. (2019, June 11). Use Your Head - Tony Buzan: The Mind Map Inventor (1974). YouTube. Retrieved 17 October 2022, from https://www.youtube.com/watch?v=EgG8GuQHHIs&feature=youtu.be

Manickam, D. M. (2021, March 4). The Power Of 'One': Tackling One Day, Email Or Article At A Time. Forbes. https://www.forbes.com/sites/forbescommunicationscouncil/2021/03/04/the-power-of-one-tackling-one-day-email-or-article-at-a-time/?sh=2ab8aa4c6604

Holmes, L. (2017, December 7). How To Stop Sweating The Small Stuff (For Good). HuffPost. Retrieved 17

October 2022, from https://www.huffpost.com/entry/sweating-the-small-stuff_n_5804524

Goeke, N. (2022, July 28). Don't Sweat The Small Stuff Summary. Four Minute Books. Retrieved 17 October 2022, from https://fourminutebooks.com/dont-sweat-the-small-stuff-+summary/

CHAPTER NINE

Wikipedia contributors. (2022, October 13). Carol Dweck. Wikipedia. Retrieved 17 October 2022, from https://en.wikipedia.org/wiki/Carol_Dweck

Talks at Google. (2015, July 16). The Growth Mindset | Carol Dweck | Talks at Google. YouTube. Retrieved 17 October 2022, from https://www.youtube.com/watch?v=-71zdXCMU6A

Better Business Magazine. (2020, January 16). How Does Your Mindset Influence Self-Discipline? Retrieved 17 October 2022, from http://auspreneurmagazine.com.au/how-does-your-mindset-+influence-self-discipline/

https:\/\/lisadanforth.com\/author\/coach-lisa\/#author. (2016, September 8). Self-Discipline: A Mindset Shift from Push to Pull - Lisa Danforth. Lisa Danforth -. Retrieved 17 October 2022, from https://

lisadanforth.com/self-discipline-mindset-shift-push-+pull/

Yeager, D. S. (2019, August 7). A national experiment reveals where a growth mindset improves achievement. Nature. Retrieved 17 October 2022, from https://www.nature.com/articles/s41586-019-1466-y

Gleeson, B. G. (2020, August 25). 9 Powerful Ways To Cultivate Extreme Self-Discipline. Forbes. https://www.forbes.com/sites/brentgleeson/2020/08/25/8-powerful-ways-to-cultivate-extreme-self-discipline/?sh=1f6cfc59182d

Salzgeber, N. (2018, January 11). How To Use Implementation Intentions to Achieve Your Goals. NJlifehacks. Retrieved 17 October 2022, from https://www.njlifehacks.com/implementation-intentions/

Gollwitzer, P. M. G., & Sheeran, P. S. (n.d.). Implementation Intentions and Goal Achievement: A Meta-analysis of Effects and Processes. Science Direct. https://www.sciencedirect.com/science/article/abs/pii/S0065260106380021

Consulting.com. (n.d.). Retrieved 17 October 2022, from https://www.consulting.com/self-discipline

10 Ways to Do What You Don't Want to Do. (2022, April 28). Zen Habits. Retrieved 17 October 2022, from https://zenhabits.net/unwanted/

The Muse Logo. (n.d.). The Muse. Retrieved 17 October 2022, from https://www.themuse.com/advice/how-i-trick-myself-into-+doing-things-i-dont-want-to-do

Schrader, J. S. (2018, February 12). 6 Benefits of an Uncluttered Space. Psychology Today. https://www.psychologytoday.com/us/blog/in-practice/201802/6-benefits-uncluttered-space

Ross, G. (2015, December 21). 8 Traits Of A Forward Thinker. WisdomTimes. Retrieved 17 October 2022, from https://www.wisdomtimes.com/blog/forward-thinker-traits/

Günel, S. (2021, December 9). Why growing your self-respect is so important and how to do it. Medium. Retrieved 17 October 2022, from https://medium.com/swlh/why-growing-your-self-respect-is-so-important-and-how-to-do-it-dbf8a99ac70a

Practicing the Discipline of Self-Respect. (2013, March 16). Retrieved 17 October 2022, from https://martinamcgowan.com/uncategorized/practicing-+discipline-self-respect/

Milton Keynes UK
Ingram Content Group UK Ltd.
UKHW011317060224
437364UK00010B/1248